THE GOSPEL ACCORDING TO
DONALD TRUMP

edited by
Robb Ryerse

DONALD TRUMP

TABLE *of* CONTENTS

THE GOSPEL ACCORDING TO
DONALD TRUMP

INTRODUCTION

For centuries, the Gospels of Matthew, Mark, Luke, and John have told the story of Jesus—a radical teacher who uplifted the poor, welcomed the outcasts, and preached inconvenient truths about humility, compassion, and love. But what happens when you strip all of that away? What if you removed every mention of kindness, every call to repentance, every demand for faith, love, or sacrifice? What if, instead, all that remained was a Jesus who performs miracles, gains power, and becomes famous?

Welcome to *The Gospel According to Donald Trump*

Inspired by Thomas Jefferson's infamous Bible, in which he cut away the supernatural to leave behind a purely moral teacher, and Donald Trump's own God Bless the USA Bible, which seeks to merge faith with American nationalism, this project takes a different approach. Here, the Gospels have been redacted, purged of anything that does not align with the words, actions, and attitudes of Donald Trump himself.

Gone are the Sermon on the Mount, the warnings about greed, the calls to serve others, and the kingdom that Jesus said was at hand. Compassion has been erased. Humility has been stricken. Women—so often dismissed or diminished in Trump's orbit—are almost omitted entirely. The names and titles of religious and political leaders have been redacted, their identities protected.

What remains is a Gospel of spectacle, of dominance, of a Jesus who walks on water, performs miracles, and amasses followers—not because he speaks of love, but because he is powerful, famous, and, above all, winning.

This is not an attempt to rewrite history. It is an exercise in revelation. By methodically stripping away everything that contradicts Trumpism, what is left exposes the emptiness of a faith co-opted by power, celebrity, and self-interest.

This is the Good News of a different kind—the gospel of success, spectacle, and supremacy. What you are about to read is not the Gospel as you have known it.

It is the Gospel as it has been reshaped by those who claim to follow both Jesus and Trump.

Whether you find it absurd, troubling, or terrifying, one thing is clear: when you remove love from the Gospel, something else takes its place.

And that, in itself, is a revelation.

THE GOSPEL ACCORDING TO
DONALD TRUMP

SAINT MATTHEW

CHAPTER 1

1 The book of the generation of Jesus Christ, the son of David, the son of Abraham.

2 Abraham begat Isaac; and Isaac begat Jacob; and Jacob begat Judas and his brethren;

3 And Judas begat Phares and Zara ▆▆▆▆; and Phares begat Esrom; and Esrom begat Aram;

4 And Aram begat Aminadab; and Aminadab begat Naasson; and Naasson begat Salmon;

5 And Salmon begat Booz ▆▆▆▆; and Booz begat Obed ▆▆▆; and Obed begat Jesse;

6 And Jesse begat David the king; and David the king begat Solomon ▆▆▆▆▆▆;

7 And Solomon begat Roboam; and Roboam begat Abia; and Abia begat Asa;

8 And Asa begat Josaphat; and Josaphat begat Joram; and Joram begat Ozias;

9 And Ozias begat Joatham; and Joatham begat Achaz; and Achaz begat Ezekias;

10 And Ezekias begat Manasses; and Manasses begat Amon; and Amon begat Josias;

11 And Josias begat Jechonias and his brethren, about the time they were carried away to Babylon:

12 And after they were brought to Babylon, Jechonias begat Salathiel; and Salathiel begat Zorobabel;

13 And Zorobabel begat Abiud; and Abiud begat Eliakim; and Eliakim begat Azor;

14 And Azor begat Sadoc; and Sadoc begat Achim; and Achim begat Eliud;

15 And Eliud begat Eleazar; and Eleazar begat Matthan; and Matthan begat Jacob;

16 And Jacob begat Joseph the husband of Mary, of whom was born Jesus, who is called Christ.

17 So all the generations from Abraham to David *are* fourteen generations; and from David until the carrying away into Babylon *are* fourteen generations; and from the carrying away into Babylon unto Christ *are* fourteen generations.

18 ¶ Now the birth of Jesus Christ was on this wise: When as his mother Mary was espoused to Joseph, before they came together, she was found with child of the Holy Ghost.

19 Then Joseph her husband, being a just *man*, and not willing to make her a publick example, was minded to put her away privily.

20 But while he thought on these things, behold, the angel of the Lord appeared unto him in a dream, saying, Joseph, thou son of David, fear not to take unto thee Mary thy wife: for that which is conceived in her is of the Holy Ghost.

21 And she shall bring forth a son, and thou shalt call his name JESUS: ▆▆▆▆▆▆▆▆▆▆

22 Now all this was done, that it might be fulfilled which was spoken of the Lord by the prophet, saying,

23 Behold, a virgin shall be with child, and shall bring forth a son, and they shall call his name Emmanuel, which being interpreted is, God with us.

24 Then Joseph being raised from sleep did as the angel of the Lord had bidden him, and took unto him his wife:

25 And knew her not till she had brought forth her firstborn son: and he called his name JESUS.

CHAPTER 2

1 Now when Jesus was born in Bethlehem of Judaea in the days of ▆▆▆▆▆▆▆, behold, there came wise men from the east to Jerusalem,

2 Saying, Where is he that is born King of the Jews? for we have seen his star in the east, and are come to worship him.

3 When ▆▆▆▆▆▆ had heard *these things*, he was troubled, and all Jerusalem with him.

4 And when he had gathered all ▆▆▆▆▆▆▆▆▆ ▆▆▆▆▆▆ together, he demanded of them where Christ should be born.

5 And they said unto him, In Bethlehem of Judaea: for thus it is written by the prophet,

6 And thou Bethlehem, *in* the land of Juda, art not the least among the princes of Juda: for out of thee shall come a Governor, that shall rule my people Israel.

7 Then ▆▆▆▆, when he had privily called the wise men, enquired of them diligently what time the star appeared.

8 And he sent them to Bethlehem, and said, Go and search diligently for the young child; and when ye have found *him*, bring me word again, that I may come and worship him also.

9 When they had heard ▆▆▆▆▆, they departed; and, lo, the star, which they saw in the east, went before them, till it came and stood over where the young child was.

10 When they saw the star, they rejoiced with exceeding great joy.

11 ¶ And when they were come into the house, they saw the young child with Mary his mother, and fell down, and worshipped him: and when they had opened their treasures, they presented unto him gifts; gold, and frankincense, and myrrh.

SAINT MATTHEW

23 And he came and dwelt in a city called Nazareth: that it might be fulfilled which was spoken by the prophets, He shall be called a Nazarene.

CHAPTER 3

1 In those days came John the Baptist, preaching in the wilderness of Judaea,
2 And saying,

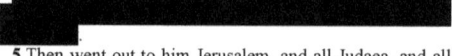

3 For this is he that was spoken of by the prophet Esaias, saying, The voice of one crying in the wilderness, Prepare ye the way of the Lord, make his paths straight.

5 Then went out to him Jerusalem, and all Judaea, and all the region round about Jordan,
6 And were baptized of him in Jordan, ▮ their sins.
7 ¶ But when he saw many of ▮ come to his baptism, he said unto them,

9 And think not to say within yourselves, We have Abraham to *our* father: for I say unto you, that God is able of these stones to raise up children unto Abraham.
10 And now also the axe is laid unto the root of the trees: therefore every tree which bringeth not forth good fruit is hewn down, and cast into the fire.
11 I indeed baptize you with water ▮ but he that cometh after me is mightier than I, whose shoes I am not worthy to bear: he shall baptize you with the Holy Ghost, and *with* fire:
12 Whose fan *is* in his hand, and he will throughly purge his floor, and gather his wheat into the garner; but he will burn up the chaff with unquenchable fire.
13 ¶ Then cometh Jesus from Galilee to Jordan unto John, to be baptized of him.
14 But John forbad him, saying, I have need to be baptized of thee, and comest thou to me?
15 And Jesus answering said unto him, Suffer *it to be so* now: ▮ Then he suffered him.
16 And Jesus, when he was baptized, went up straightway out of the water: and, lo, the heavens were opened unto him, and he saw the Spirit of God descending like a dove, and lighting upon him:
17 And lo a voice from heaven, saying, This is my beloved Son, in whom I am well pleased.

CHAPTER 4

1 Then was Jesus led up of the Spirit into the wilderness to be tempted of the devil.
2 And when he had fasted forty days and forty nights, he was afterward an hungred.
3 And when the tempter came to him, he said, If thou be the Son of God, command that these stones be made bread.

5 Then the devil taketh him up into the holy city, and setteth him on a pinnacle of the temple,
6 And saith unto him, If thou be the Son of God, cast thyself down: for it is written, He shall give his angels charge concerning thee: and in *their* hands they shall bear thee up, lest at any time thou dash thy foot against a stone.

8 Again, the devil taketh him up into an exceeding high mountain, and sheweth him all the kingdoms of the world, and the glory of them;
9 And saith unto him, All these things will I give thee, if thou wilt fall down and worship me.

11 Then the devil leaveth him, and, behold, angels came and ministered unto him.
12

13 And leaving Nazareth, he came and dwelt in Capernaum, which is upon the sea coast, in the borders of Zabulon and Nephthalim:
14 That it might be fulfilled which was spoken by Esaias the prophet, saying,
15 The land of Zabulon, and the land of Nephthalim, *by* the way of the sea, beyond Jordan, Galilee of the Gentiles;
16 The people ▮ saw great light; and to them which sat in the region and shadow of death light is sprung up.
17 ¶ From that time Jesus began to preach, and to say,

18 ¶ And Jesus, walking by the sea of Galilee, saw two brethren, Simon called Peter, and Andrew his brother, casting a net into the sea: for they were fishers.
19 And he saith unto them, Follow me, and I will make you fishers of men.
20 And they straightway left *their* nets, and followed him.
21 And going on from thence, he saw other two brethren, James *the son* of Zebedee, and John his brother, in a ship with Zebedee their father, mending their nets; and he called them.
22 And they immediately left the ship and their father, and followed him.
23 ¶ And Jesus went about all Galilee, teaching in their synagogues, and ▮ and healing all manner of sickness and all manner of disease among the people.
24 And his fame went throughout all Syria: and they brought unto him all sick people that were taken with divers diseases and torments, and those which were possessed with devils, and those which were lunatick, and those that had the palsy; and he healed them.
25 And there followed him great multitudes of people from Galilee, and *from* Decapolis, and *from* Jerusalem, and *from* Judaea, and *from* beyond Jordan.

CHAPTER 5

1 And seeing the multitudes, he went up into a mountain: and when he was set, his disciples came unto him:

2 And he opened his mouth, and taught them, saying,

CHAPTER 6

9 After this manner therefore pray ye: Our Father which art in heaven, Hallowed be thy name.

11 Give us this day our daily bread.

CHAPTER 7

and the prophets.

for this is the law

15 And he touched her hand, and the fever left her: and she arose, and ministered unto them.

16 ¶ When the even was come, they brought unto him many that were possessed with devils: and he cast out the spirits with *his* word, and healed all that were sick:

17 That it might be fulfilled which was spoken by Esaias the prophet, saying, ███████████████

18 ¶ Now when Jesus saw great multitudes about him, he gave commandment to depart unto the other side.

19 And a certain ████ came, and said unto him, Master, I will follow thee whithersoever thou goest.

21 And another of his disciples said unto him, Lord, suffer me first to go and bury my father.

23 ¶ And when he was entered into a ship, his disciples followed him.

24 And, behold, there arose a great tempest in the sea, insomuch that the ship was covered with the waves: but he was asleep.

25 And his disciples came to *him*, and awoke him, saying, Lord ████: we perish.

26 And he saith unto them, ██████████ ████████ Then he arose, and rebuked the winds and the sea; and there was a great calm.

27 But the men marvelled, saying, What manner of man is this, that even the winds and the sea obey him!

28 ¶ And when he was come to the other side into the country of the Gergesenes, there met him two possessed with devils, coming out of the tombs, exceeding fierce, so that no man might pass by that way.

29 And, behold, they cried out, saying, What have we to do with thee, Jesus, thou Son of God? art thou come hither to torment us before the time?

30 And there was a good way off from them an herd of many swine feeding.

31 So the devils besought him, saying, If thou cast us out, suffer us to go away into the herd of swine.

32 And he said unto them, Go. And when they were come out, they went into the herd of swine: and, behold, the whole herd of swine ran violently down a steep place into the sea, and perished in the waters.

33 And they that kept them fled, and went their ways into the city, and told every thing, and what was befallen to the possessed of the devils.

34 And, behold, the whole city came out to meet Jesus: and when they saw him, they besought *him* that he would depart out of their coasts.

28 And it came to pass, when Jesus had ended these sayings, the people were astonished at his doctrine:

29 For he taught them as *one* having authority, ████

CHAPTER 8

1 When he was come down from the mountain, great multitudes followed him.

2 And, behold, there came a leper and worshipped him, saying, Lord, if thou wilt, thou canst make me clean.

3 And Jesus put forth *his* hand, and touched him, saying, I will; be thou clean. And immediately his leprosy was cleansed.

4 And Jesus saith unto him, See thou tell no man; but go thy way, shew thyself to the priest, and offer the gift that Moses commanded, for a testimony unto them.

5 ¶ And when Jesus was entered into Capernaum, there came unto him a centurion, beseeching him,

6 And saying, Lord, my servant lieth at home sick of the palsy, grievously tormented.

7 And Jesus saith unto him, I will come and heal him.

8 The centurion answered and said, Lord, I am not worthy that thou shouldest come under my roof: but speak the word only, and my servant shall be healed.

9 For I am a man under authority, having soldiers under me: and I say to this *man*, Go, and he goeth; and to another, Come, and he cometh; and to my servant, Do this, and he doeth *it*.

10 When Jesus heard *it*, he marvelled, and said to them that followed, ████████████████

11 And I say unto you, That many shall come from the east and west, and shall sit down with Abraham, and Isaac, and Jacob, ██████████████

███████████ there shall be weeping and gnashing of teeth.

13 And Jesus said unto the centurion, Go thy way; ████ ████████████, *so* be it done unto thee. And his servant was healed in the selfsame hour.

14 ¶ And when Jesus was come into Peter's house, he saw his wife's mother laid, and sick of a fever.

CHAPTER 9

1 And he entered into a ship, and passed over, and came into his own city.

2 And, behold, they brought to him a man sick of the palsy, lying on a bed: and Jesus ████████████ said unto the sick of the palsy; Son, be of good cheer; ████████

3 And, behold, certain of ████████ said within themselves,

4 And Jesus knowing their thoughts said, ████████

5

or to say, Arise, and walk?

(then saith he to the sick of the palsy,) Arise, take up thy bed, and go unto thine house.

7 And he arose, and departed to his house.

8 But when the multitudes saw *it*, they marvelled, and glorified God, which had given such power unto men.

9 ¶ And as Jesus passed forth from thence, he saw a man, named Matthew, sitting at the receipt of custom: and he saith unto him, Follow me. And he arose, and followed him.

10 ¶ And it came to pass, as Jesus sat at meat in the house, behold, many publicans and ▆▆ came and sat down with him and his disciples.

11 And when ▆▆▆▆ saw *it*, they said unto his disciples, Why eateth your Master with publicans ▆▆ ▆▆?

12 But when Jesus heard *that*, he said unto them,

14 ¶ Then came to him the disciples of John, saying, Why do we and ▆▆▆▆ fast oft, but thy disciples fast not?

15 And Jesus said unto them, Can the children of the bridechamber mourn, as long as the bridegroom is with them? but the days will come, when the bridegroom shall be taken from them, and then shall they fast.

18 ¶ While he spake these things unto them, behold, there came a certain ruler, and worshipped him, saying, My daughter is even now dead: but come and lay thy hand upon her, and she shall live.

19 And Jesus arose, and followed him, and *so did* his disciples.

23 And when Jesus came into the ruler's house, and saw the minstrels and the people making a noise,

24 He said unto them, Give place: for the maid is not dead, but sleepeth. And they laughed him to scorn.

25 But when the people were put forth, he went in, and took her by the hand, and the maid arose.

26 And the fame hereof went abroad into all that land.

27 ¶ And when Jesus departed thence, two blind men followed him, crying, and saying, *Thou* Son of David, ▆▆

28 And when he was come into the house, the blind men came to him: and Jesus saith unto them,

29 Then touched he their eyes, saying,

30 And their eyes were opened; and Jesus straitly charged them, saying, ▆▆▆▆

31 But they, when they were departed, spread abroad his fame in all that country.

32 ¶ As they went out, behold, they brought to him a dumb man possessed with a devil.

33 And when the devil was cast out, the dumb spake: and the multitudes marvelled, saying, It was never so seen in Israel.

34 But ▆▆▆▆ said, He casteth out devils through the prince of the devils.

35 And Jesus went about all the cities and villages, teaching in their synagogues, ▆▆▆▆ ▆▆▆▆ and healing every sickness and every disease among the people.

36 ¶ But when he saw the multitudes,

37 Then saith he unto his disciples,

38 Pray ye therefore the Lord

CHAPTER 10

1 And when he had called unto *him* his twelve disciples, he gave them power *against* unclean spirits, to cast them out, and to heal all manner of sickness and all manner of disease.

2 Now the names of the twelve apostles are these; The first, Simon, who is called Peter, and Andrew his brother; James *the son* of Zebedee, and John his brother;

3 Philip, and Bartholomew; Thomas, and Matthew the publican; James *the son* of Alphaeus, and Lebbaeus, whose surname was Thaddaeus;

4 Simon the Canaanite, and Judas Iscariot, ▆▆▆▆

5 These twelve Jesus sent forth, and commanded them, saying, Go not into the way of the Gentiles, and into *any* city of the Samaritans enter ye not:

6 But go rather to the lost sheep of the house of Israel.

7 And as ye go, preach, saying, ▆▆▆▆

8 Heal the sick, cleanse the lepers, raise the dead, cast out devils:

for the workman is worthy of his meat.

11 And into whatsoever city or town ye shall enter, enquire who in it is worthy; and there abide till ye go thence.

12 And when ye come into an house, salute it.

13 And if the house be worthy, let your peace come upon it: but if it be not worthy, let your peace return to you.

14 And whosoever shall not receive you, nor hear your words, when ye depart out of that house or city, shake off the dust of your feet.

15 Verily I say unto you, It shall be more tolerable for the land of Sodom and Gomorrha in the day of judgment, than for that city.

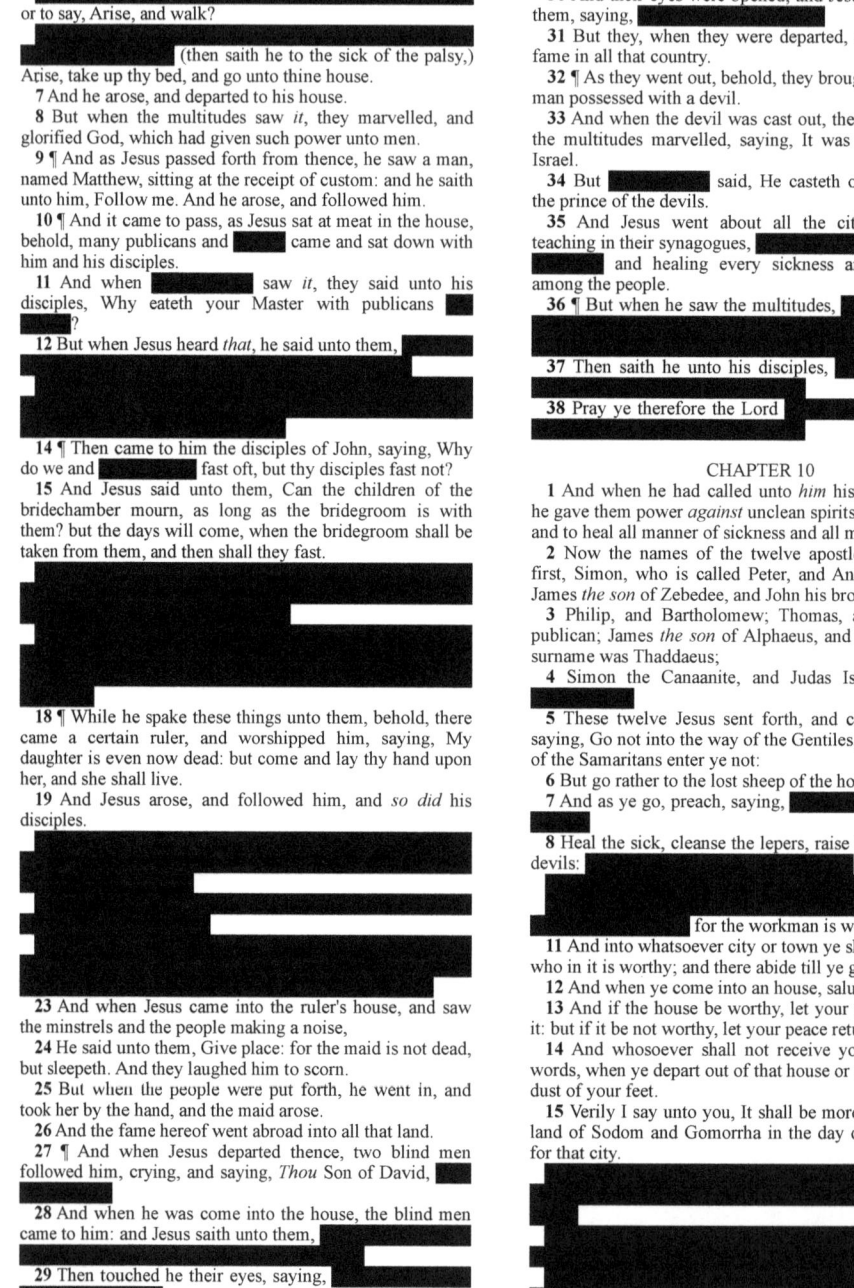

19 But when they deliver you up, take no thought how or what ye shall speak: for it shall be given you in that same hour what ye shall speak.

20 For it is not ye that speak, but the Spirit of your Father which speaketh in you.

29 Are not two sparrows sold for a farthing?

3 And said unto him, Art thou he that should come, or do we look for another?

4 Jesus answered and said unto them,

7 ¶ And as they departed, Jesus began to say unto the multitudes concerning John, What went ye out into the wilderness to see? A reed shaken with the wind?

8 But what went ye out for to see?

15 He that hath ears to hear, let him hear.

18 For John came neither eating nor drinking, and they say, He hath a devil.

19 The Son of man came eating and drinking, and they say, Behold a man gluttonous, and a winebibber, a friend of publicans

CHAPTER 11

1 And it came to pass, when Jesus had made an end of commanding his twelve disciples, he departed thence

2 Now when John had heard   the works of Christ, he sent two of his disciples,

CHAPTER 12

1 At that time Jesus went on the sabbath day through the corn; and his disciples were an hungred, and began to pluck the ears of corn, and to eat.

2 But when ▮▮▮▮▮▮▮▮ saw *it*, they said unto him, Behold, thy disciples do that which is not lawful to do upon the sabbath day.

3 But he said unto them, Have ye not read what David did, when he was an hungred, and they that were with him;

4 How he entered into the house of God, and did eat the shewbread, which was not lawful for him to eat, neither for them which were with him, but only for the priests?

5 Or have ye not read in the law, how that on the sabbath days the priests in the temple profane the sabbath, and are blameless?

9 And when he was departed thence, he went into their synagogue:

10 ¶ And, behold, there was a man which had *his* hand withered. And they asked him, saying, Is it lawful to heal on the sabbath days? that they might accuse him.

11 And he said unto them, What man shall there be among you, that shall have one sheep, and if it fall into a pit on the sabbath day, will he not lay hold on it, and lift *it* out?

13 Then saith he to the man, Stretch forth thine hand. And he stretched *it* forth; and it was restored whole, like as the other.

▮▮▮▮▮▮▮▮▮▮▮▮▮▮▮ he withdrew himself from thence: and great multitudes followed him, and he healed them all;

17 That it might be fulfilled which was spoken by Esaias the prophet, saying,

22 ¶ Then was brought unto him one possessed with a devil, blind, and dumb: and he healed him, insomuch that the blind and dumb both spake and saw.

23 And all the people were amazed, and said, Is not this the son of David?

24 But when ▮▮▮▮▮▮▮ heard *it*, they said, This *fellow* doth not cast out devils, but by Beelzebub the prince of the devils.

25 And Jesus knew their thoughts, and said unto them,

36 But I say unto you,

38 ¶ Then certain ▮▮▮▮▮▮ answered, saying, Master, we would see a sign from thee.

39 But he answered and said unto them,

8

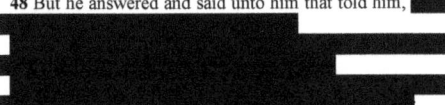

46 ¶ While he yet talked to the people, behold, *his* mother and his brethren stood without, desiring to speak with him.

47 Then one said unto him, Behold, thy mother and thy brethren stand without, desiring to speak with thee.

48 But he answered and said unto him that told him,

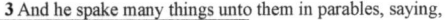

CHAPTER 13

1 The same day went Jesus out of the house, and sat by the sea side.

2 And great multitudes were gathered together unto him, so that he went into a ship, and sat; and the whole multitude stood on the shore.

3 And he spake many things unto them in parables, saying,

9 Who hath ears to hear, let him hear.

10 And the disciples came, and said unto him, Why speakest thou unto them in parables?

11 He answered and said unto them,

24 ¶ Another parable put he forth unto them, saying,

31 ¶ Another parable put he forth unto them, saying,

33 ¶ Another parable spake he unto them;

34 All these things spake Jesus unto the multitude in parables; and without a parable spake he not unto them:

35 That it might be fulfilled which was spoken by the prophet, saying, I will open my mouth in parables; I will utter things which have been kept secret from the foundation of the world.

36 Then Jesus sent the multitude away, and went into the house: and his disciples came unto him, saying,

37 He answered and said unto them,

51 Jesus saith unto them, Have ye understood all these things? They say unto him, Yea, Lord.

53 ¶ And it came to pass, *that* when Jesus had finished these parables, he departed thence.

54 And when he was come into his own country, he taught them in their synagogue, insomuch that they were astonished, and said, Whence hath this *man* this wisdom, and *these* mighty works?

55 Is not this the carpenter's son? is not his mother called Mary? and his brethren, James, and Joses, and Simon, and Judas?

56 And his sisters, are they not all with us? Whence then hath this *man* all these things?

CHAPTER 14

15 ¶ And when it was evening, his disciples came to him, saying, This is a desert place, and the time is now past; send the multitude away, that they may go into the villages, and buy themselves victuals.

16 But Jesus said unto them,

22 ¶ And straightway Jesus constrained his disciples to get into a ship, and to go before him unto the other side, while he sent the multitudes away.

23 And when he had sent the multitudes away, he went up into a mountain apart to pray: and when the evening was come, he was there alone.

24 But the ship was now in the midst of the sea, tossed with waves: for the wind was contrary.

25 And in the fourth watch of the night Jesus went unto them, walking on the sea.

26 And when the disciples saw him walking on the sea, saying, It is a spirit;

27 But straightway Jesus spake unto them, saying, it is I;

28 And Peter answered him and said, Lord, if it be thou, bid me come unto thee on the water.

29 And he said, Come. And when Peter was come down out of the ship, he walked on the water, to go to Jesus.

30 But when he saw the wind boisterous, and beginning to sink, he cried, saying,

31 And immediately Jesus stretched forth *his* hand, and caught him, and said unto him,

32 And when they were come into the ship, the wind ceased.

33 Then they that were in the ship came and worshipped him, saying, Of a truth thou art the Son of God.

34 ¶ And when they were gone over, they came into the land of Gennesaret.

35 And when the men of that place had knowledge of him, they sent out into all that country round about, and brought unto him all that were diseased;

36 And besought him that they might only touch the hem of his garment: and as many as touched were made perfectly whole.

CHAPTER 15

1 Then came to Jesus ▮▮▮▮▮▮▮▮ saying,

2 Why do thy disciples transgress the tradition ▮▮▮▮? for they wash not their hands when they eat bread.

3 But he answered and said unto them, Why do ye also transgress the commandment of God by your tradition?

10 ¶ And he called the multitude, and said unto them, Hear, and understand:

12 Then came his disciples, and said unto him,

15 Then answered Peter and said unto him, Declare unto us this parable.

16 And Jesus said, Are ye also yet without understanding?

21 ¶ Then Jesus went thence, and departed into the coasts of Tyre and Sidon.

29 And Jesus departed from thence, and came nigh unto the sea of Galilee; and went up into a mountain, and sat down there.

30 And great multitudes came unto him, having with them *those that were* lame, blind, dumb, maimed, and many others, and cast them down at Jesus' feet; and he healed them:

31 Insomuch that the multitude wondered, when they saw the dumb to speak, the maimed to be whole, the lame to walk, and the blind to see: and they glorified the God of Israel.

32 ¶ Then Jesus called his disciples *unto him*, and said,

35 And he commanded the multitude to sit down on the ground.

39 And he sent away the multitude, and took ship, and came into the coasts of Magdala.

CHAPTER 16

1 ▮▮▮▮▮▮▮▮▮▮▮▮▮ came, and tempting desired him that he would shew them a sign from heaven.

2 He answered and said unto them, When it is evening, ye say, *It will be* fair weather: for the sky is red.

3 And in the morning, *It will be* foul weather to day: for the sky is red and lowring.

5 And when his disciples were come to the other side, they had forgotten to take bread.

6 ¶ Then Jesus said unto them,

7 And they reasoned among themselves, saying, *It is* because we have taken no bread.

8 *Which* when Jesus perceived, he said unto them, ▮▮▮▮ why reason ye among yourselves, because ye have brought no bread?

9 Do ye not yet understand, neither remember the five loaves of the five thousand, and how many baskets ye took up?

10 Neither the seven loaves of the four thousand, and how many baskets ye took up?

13 ¶ When Jesus came into the coasts of Caesarea Philippi, he asked his disciples, saying, Whom do men say that I the Son of man am?

14 And they said, Some *say that thou art* John the Baptist: some, Elias; and others, Jeremias, or one of the prophets.

15 He saith unto them, But whom say ye that I am?

16 And Simon Peter answered and said, Thou art the Christ, the Son of the living God.

17 And Jesus answered and said unto him, Blessed art thou, Simon Bar-jona: for flesh and blood hath not revealed *it* unto thee, but my Father which is in heaven.

18 And I say also unto thee,

21 ¶ From that time forth began Jesus to shew unto his disciples, how that he must go unto Jerusalem, and suffer many things ▇▇▇▇▇▇▇▇▇, and be killed, and be raised again the third day.

22 Then Peter took him, and began to rebuke him, saying, Be it far from thee, Lord: this shall not be unto thee.

23 But he turned, and said unto Peter,

24 ¶ Then said Jesus unto his disciples,

CHAPTER 17

1 And after six days Jesus taketh Peter, James, and John his brother, and bringeth them up into an high mountain apart,

2 And was transfigured before them: and his face did shine as the sun, and his raiment was white as the light.

3 And, behold, there appeared unto them Moses and Elias talking with him.

4 Then answered Peter, and said unto Jesus, Lord, it is good for us to be here: if thou wilt, let us make here three tabernacles; one for thee, and one for Moses, and one for Elias.

5 While he yet spake, behold, a bright cloud overshadowed them: and behold a voice out of the cloud, which said, This is my beloved Son, in whom I am well pleased; hear ye him.

6 And when the disciples heard *it*, they fell on their face

7 And Jesus came and touched them, and said, Arise▇

8 And when they had lifted up their eyes, they saw no man, save Jesus only.

9 And as they came down from the mountain, Jesus charged them, saying,

10 And his disciples asked him, saying, Why then say ▇ ▇ that Elias must first come?

11 And Jesus answered and said unto them, Elias truly shall first come, and restore all things.

12 But I say unto you,

13 Then the disciples understood that he spake unto them of John the Baptist.

14 ¶ And when they were come to the multitude, there came to him a *certain* man, kneeling down to him, and saying,

▇▇▇▇▇▇▇▇ for he is lunatick, and sore vexed: for ofttimes he falleth into the fire, and oft into the water.

16 And I brought him to thy disciples, and they could not cure him.

17 Then Jesus answered and said,

▇▇▇▇ and he departed out of him: and the child was cured from that very hour.

19 Then came the disciples to Jesus apart, and said, Why could not we cast him out?

20 And Jesus said unto them,

22 ¶ And while they abode in Galilee, Jesus said unto them, The Son of man shall be betrayed into the hands of men:

23 And they shall kill him, and the third day he shall be raised again.

CHAPTER 18

1 At the same time came the disciples unto Jesus, saying,

21 ¶ Then came Peter to him, and said,

CHAPTER 19

1 And it came to pass, *that* when Jesus had finished these sayings, he departed from Galilee, and came into the coasts of Judaea beyond Jordan;

2 And great multitudes followed him; and he healed them there.

it is not good to marry.

and the disciples rebuked them.

14 But Jesus said,

13

and departed thence.

CHAPTER 20

17 ¶ And Jesus going up to Jerusalem took the twelve disciples apart in the way, and said unto them,

18 Behold, we go up to Jerusalem; and the Son of man shall be betrayed ▉ and they shall condemn him to death,

19 And shall deliver him ▉ to mock, and to scourge, and to crucify *him*: and the third day he shall rise again.

20 ¶ Then came to him the mother of Zebedee's children with her sons, worshipping *him*, and desiring a certain thing of him.

21 And he said unto her, What wilt thou? She saith unto him,

29 And as they departed from Jericho, a great multitude followed him.

30 ¶ And, behold, two blind men sitting by the way side, when they heard that Jesus passed by, cried out, saying, ▉ O Lord, *thou* Son of David.

31 And the multitude rebuked them, because they should hold their peace: but they cried the more, saying, ▉ O Lord, *thou* Son of David.

32 And Jesus stood still, and called them, and said, What will ye that I shall do unto you?

33 They say unto him, Lord, that our eyes may be opened.

34 ██████████████████████████ and touched their eyes: and immediately their eyes received sight, and they followed him.

CHAPTER 21

1 And when they drew nigh unto Jerusalem, and were come to Bethphage, unto the mount of Olives, then sent Jesus two disciples,

2 Saying unto them, Go into the village over against you, and straightway ye shall find an ass tied, and a colt with her: loose *them*, and bring *them* unto me.

3 And if any *man* say ought unto you, ye shall say, The Lord hath need of them; and straightway he will send them.

4 All this was done, that it might be fulfilled which was spoken by the prophet, saying,

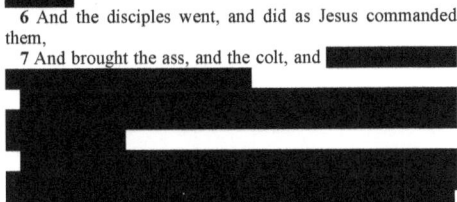

6 And the disciples went, and did as Jesus commanded them,

7 And brought the ass, and the colt, and ████

10 And when he was come into Jerusalem, all the city was moved, saying, Who is this?

11 And the multitude said, This is Jesus the prophet of Nazareth of Galilee.

14 And the blind and the lame came to him in the temple; and he healed them.

17 ¶ And he left them, and went out of the city into Bethany; and he lodged there.

18 Now in the morning as he returned into the city, he hungered.

19 And when he saw a fig tree in the way, he came to it, and found nothing thereon, but leaves only, and said unto it, Let no fruit grow on thee henceforward for ever. And presently the fig tree withered away.

20 And when the disciples saw *it*, they marvelled, saying, How soon is the fig tree withered away!

21 Jesus answered and said unto them,

23 ¶ And when he was come into the temple, ████ ████████████ the people came unto him as he was teaching, and said, By what authority doest thou these things? and who gave thee this authority?

24 And Jesus answered and said unto them, I also will ask you one thing, which if ye tell me, I in like wise will tell you by what authority I do these things.

25 The baptism of John, whence was it? from heaven, or of men? And they reasoned with themselves, saying, If we shall say, From heaven; he will say unto us, ████████ ████████

26 But if we shall say, Of men; we fear the people; for all hold John as a prophet.

27 And they answered Jesus, and said, We cannot tell. And he said unto them, Neither tell I you by what authority I do these things.

33 ¶ Hear another parable:

CHAPTER 22

1 And Jesus answered and spake unto them again by parables, and said,

16 And they sent out unto him their disciples with ▮▮▮ saying, Master, we know that thou art true, and teachest the way of God in truth,

17 Tell us therefore, What thinkest thou? Is it lawful to give tribute unto Caesar, or not?

Render therefore unto Caesar

22 When they had heard *these words*, they marvelled, and left him, and went their way.

23 ¶ The same day came to him ▮▮▮ which say that there is no resurrection, and asked him,

24 Saying, Master, Moses said, If a man die, having no children, his brother shall marry his wife, and raise up seed unto his brother.

25 Now there were with us seven brethren: and the first, when he had married a wife, deceased, and, having no issue, left his wife unto his brother:

26 Likewise the second also, and the third, unto the seventh.

27 And last of all the woman died also.

28 Therefore in the resurrection whose wife shall she be of the seven? for they all had her.

29 Jesus answered and said unto them, Ye do err, not knowing the scriptures, nor the power of God.

30 For in the resurrection they neither marry, nor are given in marriage, but are as the angels of God in heaven.

31 But as touching the resurrection of the dead, have ye not read that which was spoken unto you by God, saying,

32 I am the God of Abraham, and the God of Isaac, and the God of Jacob? God is not the God of the dead, but of the living.

33 And when the multitude heard *this*, they were astonished at his doctrine.

34 ¶ But when ▮▮▮ had heard that he had put ▮ ▮▮▮ to silence, they were gathered together.

35 Then one of them, ▮▮▮ asked *him a question,* ▮▮▮ and saying,

36 Master, which *is* the great commandment in the law?

37 Jesus said unto him, Thou shalt love the Lord thy God with all thy heart, and with all thy soul, and with all thy mind.

38 This is the first and great commandment.

41 ¶ While ▮▮▮ were gathered together, Jesus asked them,

42 Saying, What think ye of Christ? whose son is he? They say unto him, *The Son* of David.

43 He saith unto them, How then doth David in spirit call him Lord, saying,

44 The LORD said unto my Lord, Sit thou on my right hand, till I make thine enemies thy footstool?

45 If David then call him Lord, how is he his son?

46 And no man was able to answer him a word, neither durst any *man* from that day forth ask him any more *questions.*

CHAPTER 23

1 Then spake Jesus to the multitude, and to his disciples,

2 Saying,

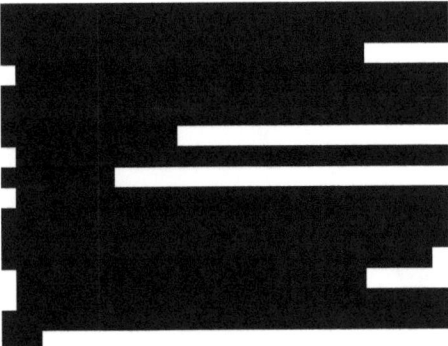

CHAPTER 24

1 And Jesus went out, and departed from the temple: and his disciples came to *him* for to shew him the buildings of the temple.

2 And Jesus said unto them, See ye not all these things?

3 ¶ And as he sat upon the mount of Olives, the disciples came unto him privately, saying, Tell us, when shall these things be? and what *shall be* the sign of thy coming, and of the end of the world?

4 And Jesus answered and said unto them,

17

CHAPTER 25

CHAPTER 26

1 And it came to pass, when Jesus had finished all these sayings, he said unto his disciples,

2 Ye know that after two days is *the feast of* the passover, and the Son of man is betrayed to be crucified.

6 ¶ Now when Jesus was in Bethany, in the house of Simon the leper,

7 There came unto him a woman having an alabaster box of very precious ointment, and poured it on his head, as he sat *at meat*.

16 And from that time he sought opportunity to betray him.

17 ¶ Now the first *day* of the *feast of* unleavened bread the disciples came to Jesus, saying unto him, Where wilt thou that we prepare for thee to eat the passover?

18 And he said, Go into the city to such a man, and say unto him, The Master saith, My time is at hand; I will keep the passover at thy house with my disciples.

19 And the disciples did as Jesus had appointed them; and they made ready the passover.

20 Now when the even was come, he sat down with the twelve.

21 And as they did eat, he said, Verily I say unto you, that one of you shall betray me.

22 And they ██████████████ and began every one of them to say unto him, Lord, is it I?

23 And he answered and said, He that dippeth *his* hand with me in the dish, the same shall betray me.

24 The Son of man goeth as it is written of him: but woe unto that man by whom the Son of man is betrayed! it had been good for that man if he had not been born.

25 Then Judas, which betrayed him, answered and said,

Master, is it I? He said unto him, Thou hast said.

26 ¶ And as they were eating, Jesus took bread, and blessed *it*, and brake *it*, and gave *it* to the disciples, and said, Take, eat; this is my body.

27 And he took the cup, and gave thanks, and gave *it* to them, saying, Drink ye all of it;

28 For this is my blood ▮▮▮▮▮▮▮▮ which is shed ▮▮▮▮▮▮▮

30 And when they had sung an hymn, they went out into the mount of Olives.

31 Then saith Jesus unto them, All ye shall be offended because of me this night: for it is written, I will smite the shepherd, and the sheep of the flock shall be scattered abroad.

32 But after I am risen again, I will go before you into Galilee.

33 Peter answered and said unto him, Though all *men* shall be offended because of thee, *yet* will I never be offended.

34 Jesus said unto him, Verily I say unto thee, That this night, before the cock crow, thou shalt deny me thrice.

35 Peter said unto him, Though I should die with thee, yet will I not deny thee. Likewise also said all the disciples.

36 ¶ Then cometh Jesus with them unto a place called Gethsemane, and saith unto the disciples, Sit ye here, while I go and pray yonder.

37 And he took with him Peter and the two sons of Zebedee, ▮▮▮▮▮▮▮▮▮▮ tarry ye here, and watch with me.

39 And he went a little further, and fell on his face, and prayed, saying, O my Father, if it be possible, let this cup pass from me: nevertheless not as I will, but as thou *wilt*.

40 And he cometh unto the disciples, and findeth them asleep, and saith unto Peter, What, could ye not watch with me one hour?

41 Watch and pray, that ye enter not into temptation: ▮▮

42 He went away again the second time, and prayed, saying, O my Father, if this cup may not pass away from me, except I drink it, thy will be done.

43 And he came and found them asleep again: for their eyes were heavy.

44 And he left them, and went away again, and prayed the third time, saying the same words.

45 Then cometh he to his disciples, and saith unto them, Sleep on now, and take *your* rest: behold, the hour is at hand, and the Son of man is betrayed ▮▮▮▮▮▮

46 Rise, let us be going: behold, he is at hand that doth betray me.

47 ¶ And while he yet spake, lo, Judas, one of the twelve, came, and with him a great multitude with swords and staves, ▮▮▮▮▮

48 Now he that betrayed him gave them a sign, saying, Whomsoever I shall kiss, that same is he: hold him fast.

49 And forthwith he came to Jesus, and said, Hail, master; and kissed him.

50 And Jesus said unto him, Friend, wherefore art thou come? Then came they, and laid hands on Jesus, and took him.

51 And, behold, one of them which were with Jesus

stretched out *his* hand, and drew his sword, and struck a servant ▮▮▮▮▮▮▮▮▮▮ and smote off his ear.

57 ¶ And they that had laid hold on Jesus led *him* away ▮▮▮▮▮▮▮▮

58 But Peter followed him afar off unto the ▮▮▮▮▮ and went in, and sat with the servants, to see the end.

60 But found none: yea, though many false witnesses came, *yet* found they none. At the last came two false witnesses,

61 And said, This *fellow* said, I am able to destroy the temple of God, and to build it in three days.

63 But Jesus held his peace. And ▮▮▮▮▮ answered and said unto him, I adjure thee by the living God, that thou tell us whether thou be the Christ, the Son of God.

64 Jesus saith unto him, Thou hast said: nevertheless I say unto you, Hereafter shall ye see the Son of man sitting on the right hand of power, and coming in the clouds of heaven.

69 ¶ Now Peter sat without in the palace: and a damsel came unto him, saying, Thou also wast with Jesus of Galilee.

70 But he denied before *them* all, saying, I know not what thou sayest.

71 And when he was gone out into the porch, another *maid* saw him, and said unto them that were there, This *fellow* was also with Jesus of Nazareth.

72 And again he denied with an oath, I do not know the man.

73 And after a while came unto *him* they that stood by, and said to Peter, Surely thou also art *one* of them; for thy speech bewrayeth thee.

74 Then began he to curse and to swear, *saying*, I know not the man. And immediately the cock crew.

75 And Peter remembered the word of Jesus, which said unto him, Before the cock crow, thou shalt deny me thrice. ▮▮▮▮▮▮▮

SAINT MATTHEW

CHAPTER 27

1 When the morning was come, ████████████ ████████████ took counsel against Jesus to put him to death:

2 And when they had bound him, they led *him* away, ███

3 ¶ Then Judas, which had betrayed him, when he saw that he was condemned, ████████████

9 Then was fulfilled that which was spoken by Jeremy the prophet, saying, And they took the thirty pieces of silver, the price of him that was valued, whom they of the children of Israel did value;

10 And gave them for the potter's field, as the Lord appointed me.

11 And Jesus stood before ████████████: and ████████████ asked him, saying, Art thou the King of the Jews? And Jesus said unto him, Thou sayest.

12 And when he was accused ████████████ he answered nothing.

13 Then said ████ unto him, Hearest thou not how many things they witness against thee?

14 And he answered him to never a word; insomuch that ████████████ marvelled greatly.

15 Now at *that* feast ████████████ was wont to release unto the people a prisoner, whom they would.

16 And they had then a notable prisoner, called Barabbas.

17 Therefore when they were gathered together, ████ said unto them, Whom will ye that I release unto you? Barabbas, or Jesus which is called Christ?

19 ¶ When ████████████ his wife sent unto him, saying, Have thou nothing to do with that just man: for I have suffered many things this day in a dream because of him.

20 But ████████████ persuaded the multitude that they should ask Barabbas, and destroy Jesus.

21 ████████████ answered and said unto them, Whether of the twain will ye that I release unto you? They said, Barabbas.

22 ████ saith unto them, What shall I do then with Jesus which is called Christ? *They* all say unto him, Let him be crucified.

23 And ████████████ said, Why, what evil hath he done? But they cried out the more, saying, Let him be crucified.

24 ¶ When ████ saw that he could prevail nothing, but *that* rather a tumult was made, he took water, and washed *his* hands before the multitude, saying, I am innocent of the blood of this ████ person: see ye *to it*.

25 Then answered all the people, and said, His blood *be* on us, and on our children.

26 ¶ Then released he Barabbas unto them: and when he had scourged Jesus, he delivered *him* to be crucified.

27 Then the soldiers ████████████ took Jesus into the common hall, and gathered unto him the whole band *of soldiers*.

28 And they stripped him, and put on him a scarlet robe.

29 ¶ And when they had platted a crown of thorns, they put *it* upon his head, and a reed in his right hand: and they bowed the knee before him, and mocked him, saying, Hail, King of the Jews!

30 And they spit upon him, and took the reed, and smote him on the head.

31 And after that they had mocked him, they took the robe off from him, and put his own raiment on him, and led him away to crucify *him*.

32 And as they came out, they found a man of Cyrene, Simon by name: him they compelled to bear his cross.

33 And when they were come unto a place called Golgotha, that is to say, a place of a skull,

34 ¶ They gave him vinegar to drink mingled with gall: and when he had tasted *thereof*, he would not drink.

35 And they crucified him, and parted his garments, casting lots: that it might be fulfilled which was spoken by the prophet, They parted my garments among them, and upon my vesture did they cast lots.

36 And sitting down they watched him there;

37 And set up over his head his accusation written, THIS IS JESUS THE KING OF THE JEWS.

38 Then were there two thieves crucified with him, one on the right hand, and another on the left.

39 ¶ And they that passed by reviled him, wagging their heads,

40 And saying, Thou that destroyest the temple, and buildest *it* in three days, save thyself. If thou be the Son of God, come down from the cross.

41 Likewise also ████████████ said, ████████████ If he be the King of Israel, let him now come down from the cross, ████ ████████████ for he said, I am the Son of God.

44 The thieves also, which were crucified with him, cast the same in his teeth.

45 Now from the sixth hour there was darkness over all the land unto the ninth hour.

46 And about the ninth hour Jesus cried with a loud voice, saying, Eli, Eli, lama sabachthani? that is to say, My God, my God, why hast thou forsaken me?

47 Some of them that stood there, when they heard *that*, said, This *man* calleth for Elias.

48 And straightway one of them ran, and took a spunge, and filled *it* with vinegar, and put *it* on a reed, and gave him to drink.

49 The rest said, Let be, let us see whether Elias will come ████████████

50 ¶ Jesus, when he had cried again with a loud voice, yielded up the ghost.

51 ████████████ ████████████ and the earth did quake, and the rocks rent;

52 And the graves were opened; and many bodies of the saints which slept arose,

53 And came out of the graves after his resurrection, and went into the holy city, and appeared unto many.

54 Now when the centurion, and they that were with him, watching Jesus, saw the earthquake, and those things that were done, ████████████ saying, Truly this was the Son of God.

55 And many women were there beholding afar off, which followed Jesus from Galilee, ministering unto him:

56 Among which was Mary Magdalene, and Mary the mother of James and Joses, and the mother of Zebedee's children.

57 When the even was come, there came a rich man of Arimathaea, named Joseph, who also himself was Jesus' disciple:

58 He went to ████ and begged the body of Jesus. Then ████ commanded the body to be delivered.

59 And when Joseph had taken the body, he wrapped it in a clean linen cloth,

60 And laid it in his own new tomb, which he had hewn out in the rock: and he rolled a great stone to the door of the sepulchre, and departed.

61 And there was Mary Magdalene, and the other Mary, sitting over against the sepulchre.

62 ¶ Now the next day, that followed the day of the preparation, ████████████████ came together unto ████

63 Saying, Sir, we remember that that deceiver said, while he was yet alive, After three days I will rise again.

64 Command therefore that the sepulchre be made sure until the third day, lest his disciples come by night, and steal him away, and say unto the people, He is risen from the dead: so the last error shall be worse than the first.

65 ████ said unto them, Ye have a watch: go your way, make *it* as sure as ye can.

66 So they went, and made the sepulchre sure, sealing the stone, and setting a watch.

CHAPTER 28

1 In the end of the sabbath, as it began to dawn toward the first *day* of the week, came Mary Magdalene and the other Mary to see the sepulchre.

2 And, behold, there was a great earthquake: for the angel of the Lord descended from heaven, and came and rolled back the stone from the door, and sat upon it.

3 His countenance was like lightning, and his raiment white as snow:

4 And for fear of him the keepers did shake, and became as dead *men*.

5 And the angel answered and said unto the women, ████ ████ for I know that ye seek Jesus, which was crucified.

6 He is not here: for he is risen, as he said. Come, see the place where the Lord lay.

11 ¶ Now when they were going, behold, some of the watch came into the city, and shewed unto ████████

all the things that were done.

████████████████████████████ and had taken counsel, they gave large money unto the soldiers,

13 Saying, Say ye, His disciples came by night, and stole him *away* while we slept.

14 And if this come to ████████'s ears, we will persuade him, and secure you.

15 So they took the money, and did as they were taught: and this saying is commonly reported ████████ until this day.

16 ¶ Then the eleven disciples went away into Galilee, into a mountain where Jesus had appointed them.

17 And when they saw him, they worshipped him: ██

18 And Jesus came and spake unto them, saying, ██ ████████████████████████████████

████████████████████████████

Amen.

THE GOSPEL ACCORDING TO

SAINT MARK

CHAPTER 1

1 The beginning of the gospel of Jesus Christ, the Son of God;

2 As it is written in the prophets, Behold, I send my messenger before thy face, which shall prepare thy way before thee.

3 The voice of one crying in the wilderness, Prepare ye the way of the Lord, make his paths straight.

4 John did baptize in the wilderness, and preach the baptism ████████████████████████████

5 And there went out unto him all the land of Judaea, and they of Jerusalem, and were all baptized of him in the river of Jordan, ████████████

6 And John was clothed with camel's hair, and with a girdle of a skin about his loins; and he did eat locusts and wild honey;

7 And preached, saying, There cometh one mightier than I after me, the latchet of whose shoes I am not worthy to stoop down and unloose.

8 I indeed have baptized you with water: but he shall baptize you with the Holy Ghost.

9 And it came to pass in those days, that Jesus came from Nazareth of Galilee, and was baptized of John in Jordan.

10 And straightway coming up out of the water, he saw the heavens opened, and the Spirit like a dove descending upon him:

11 And there came a voice from heaven, *saying*, Thou art my beloved Son, in whom I am well pleased.

12 And immediately the Spirit driveth him into the wilderness.

13 And he was there in the wilderness forty days, tempted of Satan; and was with the wild beasts; and the angels ministered unto him.

14 ████████████████████████ Jesus came into Galilee, preaching ██████████ ██████.

15 And saying, ██████████

16 Now as he walked by the sea of Galilee, he saw Simon and Andrew his brother casting a net into the sea: for they were fishers.

17 And Jesus said unto them, Come ye after me, and I will make you to become fishers of men.

18 And straightway they forsook their nets, and followed him.

19 And when he had gone a little further thence, he saw James the *son* of Zebedee, and John his brother, who also were in the ship mending their nets.

20 And straightway he called them: and they left their father Zebedee in the ship with the hired servants, and went after him.

21 And they went into Capernaum; and straightway on the sabbath day he entered into the synagogue, and taught.

22 And they were astonished at his doctrine: for he taught them as one that had authority, and not as ████████.

23 And there was in their synagogue a man with an unclean spirit; and he cried out,

24 Saying, Let *us* alone; what have we to do with thee, thou Jesus of Nazareth? art thou come to destroy us? I know

thee who thou art, the Holy One of God.

25 And Jesus rebuked him, saying, Hold thy peace, and come out of him.

26 And when the unclean spirit had torn him, and cried with a loud voice, he came out of him.

27 And they were all amazed, insomuch that they questioned among themselves, saying, What thing is this? what new doctrine *is* this? for with authority commandeth he even the unclean spirits, and they do obey him.

28 And immediately his fame spread abroad throughout all the region round about Galilee.

29 And forthwith, when they were come out of the synagogue, they entered into the house of Simon and Andrew, with James and John.

30 But Simon's wife's mother lay sick of a fever, and anon they tell him of her.

31 And he came and took her by the hand, and lifted her up; and immediately the fever left her, and she ministered unto them.

32 And at even, when the sun did set, they brought unto him all that were diseased, and them that were possessed with devils.

33 And all the city was gathered together at the door.

34 And he healed many that were sick of divers diseases, and cast out many devils; and suffered not the devils to speak, because they knew him.

35 And in the morning, rising up a great while before day, he went out, and departed into a solitary place, and there prayed.

36 And Simon and they that were with him followed after him.

37 And when they had found him, they said unto him, All *men* seek for thee.

38 And he said unto them, Let us go into the next towns, that I may preach there also: for therefore came I forth.

39 And he preached in their synagogues throughout all Galilee, and cast out devils.

40 And there came a leper to him, beseeching him, and kneeling down to him, and saying unto him, If thou wilt, thou canst make me clean.

41 And Jesus, ████████████████ put forth *his* hand, and touched him, and saith unto him, I will; be thou clean.

42 And as soon as he had spoken, immediately the leprosy departed from him, and he was cleansed.

43 And he straitly charged him, and forthwith sent him away;

44 And saith unto him, ██████████████████████ but go thy way, shew thyself to the priest, and offer for thy cleansing those things which Moses commanded, for a testimony unto them.

45 But he went out, and began to publish *it* much, and to blaze abroad the matter, insomuch that Jesus could no more openly enter into the city, but was without in desert places: and they came to him from every quarter.

CHAPTER 2

1 And again he entered into Capernaum after *some* days; and it was noised that he was in the house.

2 And straightway many were gathered together, insomuch that there was no room to receive *them*, no, not so much as about the door: and he preached the word unto them.

3 And they come unto him, bringing one sick of the palsy, which was borne of four.

4 And when they could not come nigh unto him for the press, they uncovered the roof where he was: and when they had broken *it* up, they let down the bed wherein the sick of the palsy lay.

6 But there were certain of the scribes sitting there, and reasoning in their hearts,

8 And immediately when Jesus perceived in his spirit that they so reasoned within themselves, he said unto them, Why reason ye these things in your hearts?

11 I say unto thee, Arise, and take up thy bed, and go thy way into thine house.

12 And immediately he arose, took up the bed, and went forth before them all; insomuch that they were all amazed, and glorified God, saying, We never saw it on this fashion.

13 And he went forth again by the sea side; and all the multitude resorted unto him, and he taught them.

14 And as he passed by, he saw Levi the *son* of Alphaeus sitting at the receipt of custom, and said unto him, Follow me. And he arose and followed him.

15 And it came to pass, that, as Jesus sat at meat in his house, many publicans ████████ sat also together with Jesus and his disciples: for there were many, and they followed him.

16 And when ████████████████ saw him eat with publicans ████ they said unto his disciples, How is it that he eateth and drinketh with publicans ████ ?

17 When Jesus heard *it*, he saith unto them,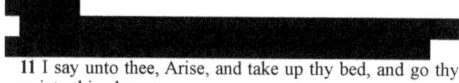

18 And the disciples of John and of ████████ used to fast: and they come and say unto him, Why do the disciples of John and of ████████ fast, but thy disciples fast not?

19 And Jesus said unto them, Can the children of the bridechamber fast, while the bridegroom is with them? as long as they have the bridegroom with them, they cannot fast.

23 And it came to pass, that he went through the corn fields on the sabbath day; and his disciples began, as they went, to pluck the ears of corn.

24 And ████████ said unto him, Behold, why do they on the sabbath day that which is not lawful?

25 And he said unto them, Have ye never read what David did, when he had need, and was an hungred, he, and they that were with him?

26 How he went into the house of God in the days of Abiathar the high priest, and did eat the shewbread, which is not lawful to eat but for the priests, and gave also to them which were with him?

CHAPTER 3

1 And he entered again into the synagogue; and there was a man there which had a withered hand.

2 And they watched him, whether he would heal him on the sabbath day; that they might accuse him.

3 And he saith unto the man which had the withered hand, Stand forth.

4 And he saith unto them, Is it lawful to do good on the sabbath days, or to do evil? to save life, or to kill? But they held their peace.

5 And when he had looked round about on ████████ he saith unto the man, Stretch forth thine hand. And he stretched *it* out: and his hand was restored whole as the other.

6 And ████████ went forth, and straightway took counsel with ████████

7 But Jesus withdrew himself with his disciples to the sea: and a great multitude from Galilee followed him, and from Judaea,

8 And from Jerusalem, and from Idumaea, and *from* beyond Jordan; and they about Tyre and Sidon, a great multitude, when they had heard what great things he did, came unto him.

9 And he spake to his disciples, that a small ship should wait on him because of the multitude, lest they should throng him.

10 For he had healed many; insomuch that they pressed upon him for to touch him, as many as had plagues.

11 And unclean spirits, when they saw him, fell down before him, and cried, saying, Thou art the Son of God.

12 And he straitly charged them that they should not make him known.

13 And he goeth up into a mountain, and calleth *unto him* whom he would: and they came unto him.

14 And he ordained twelve, that they should be with him, and that he might send them forth to preach,

15 And to have power to heal sicknesses, and to cast out devils:

16 And Simon he surnamed Peter;

17 And James the *son* of Zebedee, and John the brother of James; and he surnamed them Boanerges, which is, The sons of thunder:

18 And Andrew, and Philip, and Bartholomew, and Matthew, and Thomas, and James the *son* of Alphaeus, and Thaddaeus, and Simon the Canaanite,

19 And Judas Iscariot, which also betrayed him: and they went into an house.

20 And the multitude cometh together again, so that they could not so much as eat bread.

21 And when his friends heard *of it*, they went out to lay hold on him: for they said, He is beside himself.

22 ¶ And ████████████████

said, He hath Beelzebub, and by the prince of the devils casteth he out devils.

30 Because they said, He hath an unclean spirit.
31 ¶ There came then his brethren and his mother, and, standing without, sent unto him, calling him.
32 And the multitude sat about him, and they said unto him, Behold, thy mother and thy brethren without seek for thee.

CHAPTER 4

1 And he began again to teach by the sea side: and there was gathered unto him a great multitude, so that he entered into a ship, and sat in the sea; and the whole multitude was by the sea on the land.
2 And he taught them many things by parables, and said unto them in his doctrine,

13 And he said unto them, Know ye not this parable? and

how then will ye know all parables?

21 ¶ And he said unto them,

24 And he said unto them,

30 ¶ And he said,

33 And with many such parables spake he the word unto them, as they were able to hear *it*.
34 But without a parable spake he not unto them: and when they were alone, he expounded all things to his disciples.
35 And the same day, when the even was come, he saith unto them, Let us pass over unto the other side.
36 And when they had sent away the multitude, they took him even as he was in the ship. And there were also with him other little ships.
37 And there arose a great storm of wind, and the waves beat into the ship, so that it was now full.
38 And he was in the hinder part of the ship, asleep on a pillow: and they awake him, and say unto him, Master,

39 And he arose, and rebuked the wind, and said unto the sea, Peace, be still. And the wind ceased, and there was a great calm.

40 And he said unto them, █████████████████████

█████████████████████ and said one to another, What manner of man is this, that even the wind and the sea obey him?

CHAPTER 5

1 And they came over unto the other side of the sea, into the country of the Gadarenes.

2 And when he was come out of the ship, immediately there met him out of the tombs a man with an unclean spirit,

3 Who had *his* dwelling among the tombs; and no man could bind him, no, not with chains:

4 Because that he had been often bound with fetters and chains, and the chains had been plucked asunder by him, and the fetters broken in pieces: neither could any *man* tame him.

5 And always, night and day, he was in the mountains, and in the tombs, crying, and cutting himself with stones.

6 But when he saw Jesus afar off, he ran and worshipped him,

7 And cried with a loud voice, and said, What have I to do with thee, Jesus, *thou* Son of the most high God? I adjure thee by God, that thou torment me not.

8 For he said unto him, Come out of the man, *thou* unclean spirit.

9 And he asked him, What *is* thy name? And he answered, saying, My name *is* Legion: for we are many.

10 And he besought him much that he would not send them away out of the country.

11 Now there was there nigh unto the mountains a great herd of swine feeding.

12 And all the devils besought him, saying, Send us into the swine, that we may enter into them.

13 And forthwith Jesus gave them leave. And the unclean spirits went out, and entered into the swine: and the herd ran violently down a steep place into the sea, (they were about two thousand;) and were choked in the sea.

14 And they that fed the swine fled, and told *it* in the city, and in the country. And they went out to see what it was that was done.

15 And they come to Jesus, and see him that was possessed with the devil, and had the legion, sitting, and clothed, and in his right mind: and they were afraid.

16 And they that saw *it* told them how it befell to him that was possessed with the devil, and *also* concerning the swine.

17 And they began to pray him to depart out of their coasts.

18 And when he was come into the ship, he that had been possessed with the devil prayed him that he might be with him.

19 Howbeit Jesus suffered him not, but saith unto him, Go home to thy friends, and tell them how great things the Lord hath done for thee, ████████████

20 And he departed, and began to publish in Decapolis how great things Jesus had done for him: and all *men* did marvel.

21 And when Jesus was passed over again by ship unto the other side, much people gathered unto him: and he was nigh unto the sea.

22 And, behold, there cometh ██████████████ Jairus by name; and when he saw him, he fell at his feet,

23 And besought him greatly, saying, My little daughter lieth at the point of death: *I pray thee*, come and lay thy hands on her, that she may be healed; and she shall live.

24 And *Jesus* went with him; and much people followed him, and thronged him.

35 While he yet spake, there came from the ruler of the synagogue's *house certain* which said, Thy daughter is dead: why troublest thou the Master any further?

36 As soon as Jesus heard the word that was spoken, he saith ██████████████████████

37 And he suffered no man to follow him, save Peter, and James, and John the brother of James.

38 And he cometh to the house ██████████ ██████████ and seeth the tumult, and them that wept and wailed greatly.

39 And when he was come in, he saith unto them, Why make ye this ado, and weep? the damsel is not dead, but sleepeth.

40 And they laughed him to scorn. But when he had put them all out, he taketh the father and the mother of the damsel, and them that were with him, and entereth in where the damsel was lying.

41 And he took the damsel by the hand, and said unto her, Talitha cumi; which is, being interpreted, Damsel, I say unto thee, arise.

42 And straightway the damsel arose, and walked; for she was *of the age* of twelve years. And they were astonished with a great astonishment.

█ and commanded that something should be given her to eat.

CHAPTER 6

1 And he went out from thence, and came into his own country; and his disciples follow him.

2 And when the sabbath day was come, he began to teach in the synagogue: and many hearing *him* were astonished, saying, From whence hath this *man* these things? and what wisdom *is* this which is given unto him, that even such mighty works are wrought by his hands?

3 Is not this the carpenter, the son of Mary, the brother of James, and Joses, and of Juda, and Simon? and are not his sisters here with us?

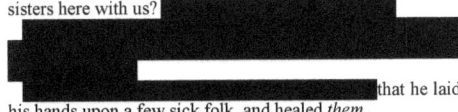

that he laid his hands upon a few sick folk, and healed *them*. And he went round about the villages, teaching.

7 ¶ And he called *unto him* the twelve, and began to send them forth by two and two; and gave them power over unclean spirits;

13 And they cast out many devils, and anointed with oil many that were sick, and healed *them*.

14 And ████████ heard *of him*; (for his name was spread abroad:) and he said, That John the Baptist was risen from the dead, and therefore mighty works do shew forth themselves in him.

15 Others said, That it is Elias. And others said, That it is a prophet, or as one of the prophets.

16 But when ████ heard *thereof*, he said, It is John, he is risen from the dead.

17 For

30 And the apostles gathered themselves together unto Jesus, and told him all things, both what they had done, and what they had taught.

31 And he said unto them, Come ye yourselves apart into a desert place, and rest a while: for there were many coming and going, and they had no leisure so much as to eat.

32 And they departed into a desert place by ship privately.

33 And the people saw them departing, and many knew him, and ran afoot thither out of all cities, and outwent them, and came together unto him.

34 And Jesus, when he came out, saw much people,

35 And when the day was now far spent, his disciples came unto him, and said, This is a desert place, and now the time *is* far passed:

36 Send them away, that they may go into the country round about, and into the villages, and buy themselves bread: for they have nothing to eat.

37 He answered and said unto them, Give ye them to eat. And they say unto him, Shall we go and buy two hundred pennyworth of bread, and give them to eat?

38 He saith unto them, How many loaves have ye? go and see. And when they knew, they say, Five, and two fishes.

39 And he commanded them to make all sit down by companies upon the green grass.

40 And they sat down in ranks, by hundreds, and by fifties.

41 And when he had taken the five loaves and the two fishes, he looked up to heaven, and blessed, and brake the loaves, and gave *them* to his disciples to set before them; and the two fishes divided he among them all.

42 And they did all eat, and were filled.

43 And they took up twelve baskets full of the fragments, and of the fishes.

44 And they that did eat of the loaves were about five thousand men.

45 And straightway he constrained his disciples to get into the ship, and to go to the other side before unto Bethsaida, while he sent away the people.

46 And when he had sent them away, he departed into a mountain to pray.

47 And when even was come, the ship was in the midst of the sea, and he alone on the land.

48 And he saw them toiling in rowing; for the wind was contrary unto them: and about the fourth watch of the night he cometh unto them, walking upon the sea, and would have passed by them.

49 But when they saw him walking upon the sea, they supposed it had been a spirit, And immediately he talked with them, and saith unto them, it is I;

51 And he went up unto them into the ship; and the wind ceased: and they were sore amazed in themselves beyond measure, and wondered.

52 For they considered not *the miracle* of the loaves:

53 And when they had passed over, they came into the land of Gennesaret, and drew to the shore.

54 And when they were come out of the ship, straightway they knew him,

55 And ran through that whole region round about, and began to carry about in beds those that were sick, where they heard he was.

56 And whithersoever he entered, into villages, or cities, or country, they laid the sick in the streets, and besought him that they might touch if it were but the border of his garment: and as many as touched him were made whole.

CHAPTER 7

1 Then came together unto him ▮

2 And when they saw some of his disciples eat bread with defiled, that is to say, with unwashen, hands, they found fault.

3 For ▮ except they wash *their* hands oft, eat not, holding the tradition ▮.

4 And *when they come* from the market, except they wash, they eat not. And many other things there be, which they have received to hold, *as* the washing of cups, and pots, brasen vessels, and of tables.

5 Then ▮ asked him, Why walk not thy disciples according to the tradition ▮, but eat bread with unwashen hands?

6 He answered and said unto them,

9 And he said unto them,

14 ¶ And when he had called all the people *unto him*, he said unto them, Hearken unto me every one *of you*, and understand:

24 ¶ And from thence he arose, and went into the borders of Tyre and Sidon, and entered into an house, and would have no man know *it*: but he could not be hid.

31 ¶ And again, departing from the coasts of Tyre and Sidon, he came unto the sea of Galilee, through the midst of the coasts of Decapolis.

32 And they bring unto him one that was deaf, and had an impediment in his speech; and they beseech him to put his hand upon him.

33 And he took him aside from the multitude, and put his fingers into his ears, and he spit, and touched his tongue;

34 And looking up to heaven, he sighed, and saith unto him, Ephphatha, that is, Be opened.

35 And straightway his ears were opened, and the string of his tongue was loosed, and he spake plain.

36 ▮

37 And were beyond measure astonished, saying, He hath done all things well: he maketh both the deaf to hear, and the dumb to speak.

CHAPTER 8

1 In those days the multitude being very great, and having nothing to eat, Jesus called his disciples *unto him*, and saith unto them,

2 I have compassion on the multitude, because they have now been with me three days, and have nothing to eat:

3 And if I send them away fasting to their own houses, they will faint by the way: for divers of them came from far.

4 And his disciples answered him, From whence can a man satisfy these *men* with bread here in the wilderness?

5 And he asked them, How many loaves have ye? And they said, Seven.

6 And he commanded the people to sit down on the ground: and he took the seven loaves, and gave thanks, and brake, and gave to his disciples to set before *them*; and they did set *them* before the people.

7 And they had a few small fishes: and he blessed, and commanded to set them also before *them*.

8 So they did eat, and were filled: and they took up of the broken *meat* that was left seven baskets.

9 And they that had eaten were about four thousand: and

28

he sent them away.

10 ¶ And straightway he entered into a ship with his disciples, and came into the parts of Dalmanutha.

11 And ███████████ came forth, and began to question with him, seeking of him a sign from heaven, tempting him.

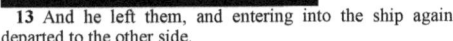
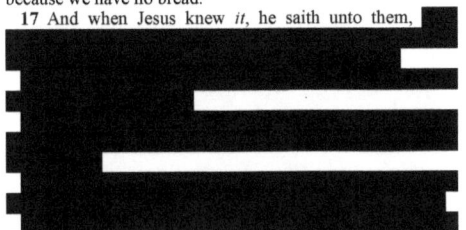

13 And he left them, and entering into the ship again departed to the other side.

14 ¶ Now *the disciples* had forgotten to take bread, neither had they in the ship with them more than one loaf.

15 And he charged them, saying, ███████

16 And they reasoned among themselves, saying, *It is* because we have no bread.

17 And when Jesus knew *it*, he saith unto them, ██

22 ¶ And he cometh to Bethsaida; and they bring a blind man unto him, and besought him to touch him.

23 And he took the blind man by the hand, and led him out of the town; and when he had spit on his eyes, and put his hands upon him, he asked him if he saw ought.

24 And he looked up, and said, I see men as trees, walking.

25 After that he put *his* hands again upon his eyes, and made him look up: and he was restored, and saw every man clearly.

26 And he sent him away to his house, saying, Neither go into the town, nor tell *it* to any in the town.

27 ¶ And Jesus went out, and his disciples, into the towns of Caesarea Philippi: and by the way he asked his disciples, saying unto them, Whom do men say that I am?

28 And they answered, John the Baptist: but some *say,* Elias; and others, One of the prophets.

29 And he saith unto them, But whom say ye that I am? And Peter answereth and saith unto him, Thou art the Christ.

31 And he began to teach them, that the Son of man must suffer many things, ███████████ and be killed, and after three days rise again.

32 And he spake that saying openly. And Peter took him, and began to rebuke him.

33 But when he had turned about and looked on his disciples, he rebuked Peter, saying, Get thee behind me, Satan:

34 ¶ And when he had called the people *unto him* with his disciples also, he said unto them,

CHAPTER 9

1 And he said unto them, ███████

2 ¶ And after six days Jesus taketh *with him* Peter, and James, and John, and leadeth them up into an high mountain apart by themselves: and he was transfigured before them.

3 And his raiment became shining, exceeding white as snow; so as no fuller on earth can white them.

4 And there appeared unto them Elias with Moses: and they were talking with Jesus.

5 And Peter answered and said to Jesus, Master, it is good for us to be here: and let us make three tabernacles; one for thee, and one for Moses, and one for Elias.

7 And there was a cloud that overshadowed them: and a voice came out of the cloud, saying, This is my beloved Son: hear him.

8 And suddenly, when they had looked round about, they saw no man any more, save Jesus only with themselves.

9 And as they came down from the mountain, ████

11 ¶ And they asked him, saying, Why say ███████ that Elias must first come?

12 And he answered and told them, Elias verily cometh first, and restoreth all things; and how it is written of the Son of man, that he must suffer many things, and be set at nought.

13 But I say unto you, That Elias is indeed come, and they have done unto him whatsoever they listed, as it is written of him.

14 ¶ And when he came to *his* disciples, he saw a great multitude about them, and ███████ questioning with them.

15 And straightway all the people, when they beheld him, were greatly amazed, and running to *him* saluted him.

16 And he asked ███████, What question ye with them?

17 And one of the multitude answered and said, Master, I have brought unto thee my son, which hath a dumb spirit;

18 And wheresoever he taketh him, he teareth him: and he foameth, and gnasheth with his teeth, and pineth away: and I spake to thy disciples that they should cast him out; and they could not.

19 He answereth him, and saith, ███████ bring him unto me.

20 And they brought him unto him: and when he saw him, straightway the spirit tare him; and he fell on the ground, and wallowed foaming.

21 And he asked his father, How long is it ago since this came unto him? And he said, Of a child.

22 And ofttimes it hath cast him into the fire, and into the waters, to destroy him: but if thou canst do any thing, ▮▮ ▮▮▮▮▮▮ and help us.

23 Jesus said unto him, ▮▮▮▮▮▮

25 When Jesus saw that the people came running together, he rebuked the foul spirit, saying unto him, *Thou* dumb and deaf spirit, I charge thee, come out of him, and enter no more into him.

26 And *the spirit* cried, and rent him sore, and came out of him: and he was as one dead; insomuch that many said, He is dead.

27 But Jesus took him by the hand, and lifted him up; and he arose.

28 And when he was come into the house, his disciples asked him privately, Why could not we cast him out?

29 And he said unto them, ▮▮▮▮▮▮

30 ¶ And they departed thence, and passed through Galilee; and he would not that any man should know *it*.

31 For he taught his disciples, and said unto them, The Son of man is delivered into the hands of men, and they shall kill him; and after that he is killed, he shall rise the third day.

32 But they understood not that saying, and were afraid to ask him.

33 ¶ And he came to Capernaum: and being in the house he asked them, What was it that ye disputed among yourselves by the way?

34 But they held their peace: for by the way they had disputed among themselves, who *should be* the greatest.

35 And he sat down, and called the twelve, and saith unto them, ▮▮▮▮▮▮

38 ¶ And John answered him, saying, Master, we saw one casting out devils in thy name, and he followeth not us: and we forbad him, because he followeth not us.

39 But Jesus said, ▮▮▮▮▮▮

CHAPTER 10

1 And he arose from thence, and cometh into the coasts of Judaea by the farther side of Jordan: and the people resort unto him again; and, as he was wont, he taught them again.

2 ¶ And ▮▮▮▮▮▮ came to him, and asked him, Is it lawful for a man to put away *his* wife? tempting him.

3 And he answered and said unto them, ▮▮▮▮▮▮

13 ¶ And they brought young children to him, that he should touch them: and *his* disciples rebuked those that brought *them*.

14 But when Jesus saw *it*, he was much displeased, and said unto them, ▮▮▮▮▮▮

17 ¶ And when he was gone forth into the way, there came one running, and kneeled to him, and asked him, Good Master, what shall I do that I may inherit eternal life?

18 And Jesus said unto him, ▮▮▮▮▮▮

29 And Jesus answered and said,

32 ¶ And they were in the way going up to Jerusalem; and Jesus went before them: and they were amazed; and as they followed, ▮▮▮ And he took again the twelve, and began to tell them what things should happen unto him,

33 *Saying*, Behold, we go up to Jerusalem; and the Son of man shall be delivered unto ▮▮▮ and they shall condemn him to death, and shall deliver him to ▮▮▮:

34 And they shall mock him, and shall scourge him, and shall spit upon him, and shall kill him: and the third day he shall rise again.

35 ¶ And James and John, the sons of Zebedee, come unto him, saying,

36 And he said unto them,

37 They said unto him,

38 But Jesus said unto them,

39 And they said unto him, ▮▮▮ And Jesus said unto them,

41 And when the ten heard *it*, they began to be much displeased with James and John.

42 But Jesus called them *to him*, and saith unto them,

46 ¶ And they came to Jericho: and as he went out of Jericho with his disciples and a great number of people, blind Bartimaeus, the son of Timaeus, sat by the highway side begging.

47 And when he heard that it was Jesus of Nazareth, he began to cry out, and say, Jesus, *thou* Son of David▮

48 And many charged him that he should hold his peace: but he cried the more a great deal, *Thou* Son of David▮

49 And Jesus stood still, and commanded him to be called. And they call the blind man, saying unto him, ▮▮▮ rise; he calleth thee.

50 And he, casting away his garment, rose, and came to Jesus.

51 And Jesus answered and said unto him, What wilt thou that I should do unto thee? The blind man said unto him, Lord, that I might receive my sight.

52 And Jesus said unto him, Go thy way; ▮▮▮ And immediately he received his sight, and followed Jesus in the way.

CHAPTER 11

1 And when they came nigh to Jerusalem, unto Bethphage and Bethany, at the mount of Olives, he sendeth forth two of his disciples,

2 And saith unto them, Go your way into the village over against you: and as soon as ye be entered into it, ye shall find a colt tied, whereon never man sat; loose him, and bring *him*.

3 And if any man say unto you, Why do ye this? say ye that the Lord hath need of him; and straightway he will send him hither.

4 And they went their way, and found the colt tied by the door without in a place where two ways met; and they loose him.

5 And certain of them that stood there said unto them, What do ye, loosing the colt?

6 And they said unto them even as Jesus had commanded: and they let them go.

11 And Jesus entered into Jerusalem, and into the temple: and when he had looked round about upon all things, and now the eventide was come, he went out unto Bethany with the twelve.

12 ¶ And on the morrow, when they were come from Bethany, he was hungry:

13 And seeing a fig tree afar off having leaves, he came, if haply he might find any thing thereon: and when he came to it, he found nothing but leaves; for the time of figs was not *yet*.

14 And Jesus answered and said unto it, No man eat fruit of thee hereafter for ever. And his disciples heard *it*.

19 And when even was come, he went out of the city.

20 ¶ And in the morning, as they passed by, they saw the fig tree dried up from the roots.

21 And Peter calling to remembrance saith unto him, Master, behold, the fig tree which thou cursedst is withered away.

22 And Jesus answering saith unto them,

27 And they come again to Jerusalem: and as he was walking in the temple, there come to him

28 And say unto him, By what authority doest thou these things? and who gave thee this authority to do these things?

29 And Jesus answered and said unto them, I will also ask of you one question, and answer me, and I will tell you by what authority I do these things.

30 The baptism of John, was *it* from heaven, or of men? answer me.

31 And they reasoned with themselves, saying, If we shall say, From heaven; he will say, Why then did ye not believe him?

32 But if we shall say, Of men; they feared the people: for all *men* counted John, that he was a prophet indeed.

33 And they answered and said unto Jesus, We cannot tell. And Jesus answering saith unto them, Neither do I tell you by what authority I do these things.

CHAPTER 12

1 And he began to speak unto them by parables.

13 ¶ And they send unto him certain of

But he, said unto them,

Render to Caesar And they marvelled at him.

18 ¶ Then come unto him which say there is no resurrection; and they asked him, saying,

19 Master, Moses wrote unto us, If a man's brother die, and leave *his* wife *behind him*, and leave no children, that his brother should take his wife, and raise up seed unto his brother.

20 Now there were seven brethren: and the first took a wife, and dying left no seed.

21 And the second took her, and died, neither left he any seed: and the third likewise.

22 And the seven had her, and left no seed: last of all the woman died also.

23 In the resurrection therefore, when they shall rise, whose wife shall she be of them? for the seven had her to wife.

24 And Jesus answering said unto them, Do ye not therefore err, because ye know not the scriptures, neither the power of God?

25 For when they shall rise from the dead, they neither marry, nor are given in marriage; but are as the angels which are in heaven.

26 And as touching the dead, that they rise: have ye not read in the book of Moses, how in the bush God spake unto him, saying, I *am* the God of Abraham, and the God of Isaac, and the God of Jacob?

27 He is not the God of the dead, but the God of the living: ye therefore do greatly err.

28 ¶ And one of came, and having heard them reasoning together, and perceiving that he had answered

them well, asked him, Which is the first commandment of all?

29 And Jesus answered him, The first of all the commandments *is*, Hear, O Israel; The Lord our God is one Lord:

30 And thou shalt love the Lord thy God with all thy heart, and with all thy soul, and with all thy mind, and with all thy strength: this *is* the first commandment.

35 ¶ And Jesus answered and said, while he taught in the temple, How say ███ that Christ is the Son of David?

36 For David himself said by the Holy Ghost, The LORD said to my Lord, Sit thou on my right hand, till I make thine enemies thy footstool.

37 David therefore himself calleth him Lord; and whence is he *then* his son? And the common people heard him gladly.

38 ¶ And he said unto them in his doctrine, █

CHAPTER 13

1 And as he went out of the temple, one of his disciples saith unto him, Master, see what manner of stones and what buildings *are here*!

2 And Jesus answering said unto him, █

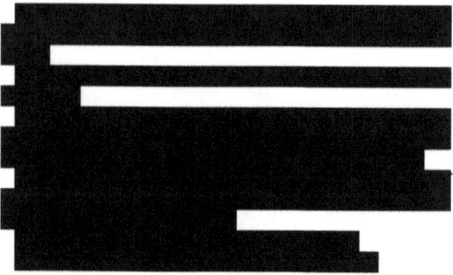

CHAPTER 14

1 After two days was *the feast of* the passover, and of unleavened bread:

3 ¶ And being in Bethany in the house of Simon the leper, as he sat at meat, there came a woman having an alabaster box of ointment of spikenard very precious; and she brake the box, and poured *it* on his head.

10 ¶ And Judas Iscariot, one of the twelve, went , to betray him unto them.
11 And when they heard *it*, they were glad, and promised to give him money. And he sought how he might conveniently betray him.
12 ¶ And the first day of unleavened bread, when they killed the passover, his disciples said unto him, Where wilt thou that we go and prepare that thou mayest eat the passover?
13 And he sendeth forth two of his disciples, and saith unto them, Go ye into the city, and there shall meet you a man bearing a pitcher of water: follow him.
14 And wheresoever he shall go in, say ye to the goodman of the house, The Master saith, Where is the guestchamber, where I shall eat the passover with my disciples?
15 And he will shew you a large upper room furnished *and* prepared: there make ready for us.
16 And his disciples went forth, and came into the city, and found as he had said unto them: and they made ready the passover.
17 And in the evening he cometh with the twelve.
18 And as they sat and did eat, Jesus said, Verily I say unto you, One of you which eateth with me shall betray me.
19 And they began to be sorrowful, and to say unto him one by one, *Is* it I? and another *said, Is* it I?
20 And he answered and said unto them, *It is* one of the twelve, that dippeth with me in the dish.

22 ¶ And as they did eat, Jesus took bread, and blessed, and brake *it*, and gave to them, and said, Take, eat: this is my body.
23 And he took the cup, and when he had given thanks, he gave *it* to them: and they all drank of it.
24 And he said unto them, This is my blood
25 Verily I say unto you, I will drink no more of the fruit of the vine,

26 ¶ And when they had sung an hymn, they went out into the mount of Olives.
27 And Jesus saith unto them, All ye shall be offended because of me this night: for it is written, I will smite the shepherd, and the sheep shall be scattered.
28 But after that I am risen, I will go before you into Galilee.
29 But Peter said unto him, Although all shall be offended, yet *will* not I.
30 And Jesus saith unto him, Verily I say unto thee, That this day, *even* in this night, before the cock crow twice, thou shalt deny me thrice.
31 But he spake the more vehemently, If I should die with thee, I will not deny thee in any wise. Likewise also said they all.
32 And they came to a place which was named Gethsemane: and he saith to his disciples, Sit ye here, while I shall pray.
33 And he taketh with him Peter and James and John, and to be very heavy;
34 And saith unto them, tarry ye here, and watch.
35 And he went forward a little, and fell on the ground, and prayed that, if it were possible, the hour might pass from him.
36 And he said, , Father, all things *are* possible unto thee; take away this cup from me: nevertheless not what I will, but what thou wilt.
37 And he cometh, and findeth them sleeping, and saith unto Peter, Simon, sleepest thou? couldest not thou watch one hour?

39 And again he went away, and prayed, and spake the same words.
40 And when he returned, he found them asleep again, (for their eyes were heavy,) neither wist they what to answer him.
41 And he cometh the third time, and saith unto them, Sleep on now, and take *your* rest: it is enough, the hour is come; behold, the Son of man is betrayed
42 Rise up, let us go; lo, he that betrayeth me is at hand.
43 ¶ And immediately, while he yet spake, cometh Judas, one of the twelve, and with him a great multitude
44 And he that betrayed him had given them a token,

saying, Whomsoever I shall kiss, that same is he; take him, and lead *him* away safely.

45 And as soon as he was come, he goeth straightway to him, and saith, Master, master; and kissed him.

46 ¶ And they laid their hands on him, and took him.

50 And they all forsook him, and fled.

51 And there followed him a certain young man, having a linen cloth cast about *his* naked *body*; and the young men laid hold on him:

52 And he left the linen cloth, and fled from them naked.

53 ¶ And they led Jesus away

54 And Peter followed him afar off, ███ and he sat with the servants, and warmed himself at the fire.

55 ███ sought for witness against Jesus to put him to death; and found none.

56 For many bare false witness against him, but their witness agreed not together.

57 And there arose certain, and bare false witness against him, saying,

58 We heard him say, I will destroy this temple that is made with hands, and within three days I will build another made without hands.

59 But neither so did their witness agree together.

60 And ███ stood up in the midst, and asked Jesus, saying, Answerest thou nothing? what *is it which* these witness against thee?

61 But he held his peace, and answered nothing. Again ███ asked him, and said unto him, Art thou the Christ, the Son of the Blessed?

62 And Jesus said, I am: and ye shall see the Son of man sitting on the right hand of power, and coming in the clouds of heaven.

63 Then ███ rent his clothes, and saith, What need we any further witnesses?

64 Ye have heard the blasphemy: what think ye? And they all condemned him to be guilty of death.

65 And some began to spit on him, and to cover his face, and to buffet him, and to say unto him, Prophesy: and the servants did strike him with the palms of their hands.

66 ¶ And as Peter was beneath ███ there cometh one of the maids of

67 And when she saw Peter warming himself, she looked upon him, and said, And thou also wast with Jesus of Nazareth.

68 But he denied, saying, I know not, neither understand I what thou sayest. And he went out into the porch; and the cock crew.

69 And a maid saw him again, and began to say to them that stood by, This is *one* of them.

70 And he denied it again. And a little after, they that stood by said again to Peter, Surely thou art *one* of them: for thou art a Galilaean, and thy speech agreeth *thereto*.

71 But he began to curse and to swear, *saying*, I know not this man of whom ye speak.

72 And the second time the cock crew. And Peter called to mind the word that Jesus said unto him, Before the cock crow twice, thou shalt deny me thrice. ███

CHAPTER 15

1 And straightway in the morning ███ , and bound Jesus, and carried *him* away, and delivered *him* to ███.

2 And ███ asked him, Art thou the King of the Jews? And he answering said unto him, Thou sayest *it*.

3 And ███ accused him of many things: but he answered nothing.

4 And ███ asked him again, saying, Answerest thou nothing? behold how many things they witness against thee.

5 But Jesus yet answered nothing; so that ███ marvelled.

6 Now at *that* feast he released unto them one prisoner, whomsoever they desired.

7 And there was *one* named Barabbas, *which lay* bound with them that had made ███ with him, who had committed murder in the ███

8 And the multitude crying aloud began to desire *him to do* as he had ever done unto them.

9 But ███ answered them, saying, Will ye that I release unto you the King of the Jews?

11 But ███ moved the people, that he should rather release Barabbas unto them.

12 And ███ answered and said again unto them, What will ye then that I shall do *unto him* whom ye call the King of the Jews?

13 And they cried out again, Crucify him.

14 Then ███ said unto them, Why, what evil hath he done? And they cried out the more exceedingly, Crucify him.

15 ¶ And so ███, willing to content the people, released Barabbas unto them, and delivered Jesus, when he had scourged *him*, to be crucified.

16 And the soldiers led him away into the hall, called Praetorium; and they call together the whole band.

17 And they clothed him with purple, and platted a crown of thorns, and put it about his *head*,

18 And began to salute him, Hail, King of the Jews!

19 And they smote him on the head with a reed, and did spit upon him, and bowing *their* knees worshipped him.

20 And when they had mocked him, they took off the purple from him, and put his own clothes on him, and led him out to crucify him.

21 And they compel one Simon a Cyrenian, who passed by, coming out of the country, the father of Alexander and Rufus, to bear his cross.

22 And they bring him unto the place Golgotha, which is, being interpreted, The place of a skull.

23 And they gave him to drink wine mingled with myrrh: but he received *it* not.

24 And when they had crucified him, they parted his garments, casting lots upon them, what every man should take.

25 And it was the third hour, and they crucified him.

26 And the superscription of his accusation was written over, THE KING OF THE JEWS.

27 And with him they crucify two thieves; the one on his

right hand, and the other on his left.

28 And the scripture was fulfilled, which saith, And he was numbered with the transgressors.

29 And they that passed by railed on him, wagging their heads, and saying, Ah, thou that destroyest the temple, and buildest *it* in three days,

33 And when the sixth hour was come, there was darkness over the whole land until the ninth hour.

34 And at the ninth hour Jesus cried with a loud voice, saying, Eloi, Eloi, lama sabachthani? which is, being interpreted, My God, my God, why hast thou forsaken me?

35 And some of them that stood by, when they heard *it*, said, Behold, he calleth Elias.

36 And one ran and filled a spunge full of vinegar, and put *it* on a reed, and gave him to drink, saying, Let alone; let us see whether Elias will come to take him down.

37 And Jesus cried with a loud voice, and gave up the ghost.

39 ¶ And when the centurion, which stood over against him, saw that he so cried out, and gave up the ghost, he said, Truly this man was the Son of God.

42 ¶ And now when the even was come, because it was the preparation, that is, the day before the sabbath,

43 Joseph of Arimathaea, an honourable counsellor, came, and went in boldly unto and craved the body of Jesus.

44 And marvelled if he were already dead: and calling *unto him* the centurion, he asked him whether he had been any while dead.

45 And when he knew *it* of the centurion, he gave the body to Joseph.

46 And he bought fine linen, and took him down, and wrapped him in the linen, and laid him in a sepulchre which was hewn out of a rock, and rolled a stone unto the door of the sepulchre.

CHAPTER 16

2 And very early in the morning the first *day* of the week, they came unto the sepulchre at the rising of the sun.

3 And they said among themselves, Who shall roll us away the stone from the door of the sepulchre?

4 And when they looked, they saw that the stone was rolled away: for it was very great.

5 And entering into the sepulchre, they saw a young man sitting on the right side, clothed in a long white garment;

6 And he saith unto them, Ye seek Jesus of Nazareth, which was crucified: he is risen; he is not here: behold the place where they laid him.

7 But go your way, tell his disciples and Peter that he goeth before you into Galilee: there shall ye see him, as he said unto you.

8 And they went out quickly, and fled from the sepulchre; for they trembled and were amazed: neither said they any thing to any *man*;

9 ¶ Now when *Jesus* was risen early the first *day* of the week,

12 ¶ After that he appeared in another form unto two of them, as they walked, and went into the country.

13 And they went and told *it* unto the residue:

14 ¶ Afterward he appeared unto the eleven as they sat at meat,

15 And he said unto them,

In my name shall they cast out devils; they shall speak with new tongues;

18 They shall take up serpents; and if they drink any deadly thing, it shall not hurt them; they shall lay hands on the sick, and they shall recover.

19 ¶ So then after the Lord had spoken unto them, he was received up into heaven,

Amen.

SAINT LUKE

CHAPTER 1

1 Forasmuch as many have taken in hand to set forth in order a declaration of those things █████████████

2 Even as they delivered them unto us, which from the beginning were eyewitnesses, and ministers of the word;

3 It seemed good to me also, having had perfect understanding of all things from the very first, to write unto thee in order, ████████████████

4 That thou mightest know the certainty of those things, wherein thou hast been instructed.

5 ¶ There was in the days of ███████████████ a certain priest named Zacharias, of the course of Abia: and his wife *was* of the daughters of Aaron, and her name *was* Elisabeth.

6 And they were both ███████ before God, walking in all the commandments and ordinances of the Lord blameless.

7 And they had no child, because that Elisabeth was barren, and they both were *now* well stricken in years.

8 And it came to pass, that while he executed the priest's office before God in the order of his course,

9 According to the custom of the priest's office, his lot was to burn incense when he went into the temple of the Lord.

10 And the whole multitude of the people were praying without at the time of incense.

11 And there appeared unto him an angel of the Lord standing on the right side of the altar of incense.

12 And when Zacharias saw *him*, ████████████████
█████████

13 But the angel said unto him, ████████ Zacharias: for thy prayer is heard; and thy wife Elisabeth shall bear thee a son, and thou shalt call his name John.

14 And thou shalt have joy and gladness; and many shall rejoice at his birth.

15 For he shall be great in the sight of the Lord, and shall drink neither wine nor strong drink; and he shall be filled with the Holy Ghost, even from his mother's womb.
████████████████████████

17 And he shall go before him in the spirit and power of Elias, ████████████████████████████████ to make ready a people prepared for the Lord.

18 And Zacharias said unto the angel, Whereby shall I know this? for I am an old man, and my wife well stricken in years.

19 And the angel answering said unto him, I am Gabriel, that stand in the presence of God; and am sent to speak unto thee, and to shew thee these glad tidings.

20 And, behold, thou shalt be dumb, and not able to speak, until the day that these things shall be performed, ██████████

21 And the people waited for Zacharias, and marvelled that he tarried so long in the temple.

22 And when he came out, he could not speak unto them: and they perceived that he had seen a vision in the temple: for he beckoned unto them, and remained speechless.

23 And it came to pass, that, as soon as the days of his ministration were accomplished, he departed to his own house.

24 And after those days his wife Elisabeth conceived, and hid herself five months, saying,

25 Thus hath the Lord dealt with me in the days wherein he looked on *me*, to take away my reproach among men.

26 And in the sixth month the angel Gabriel was sent from God unto a city of Galilee, named Nazareth,

27 To a virgin espoused to a man whose name was Joseph, of the house of David; and the virgin's name *was* Mary.

28 And the angel came in unto her, and said, Hail, *thou that art* highly favoured, the Lord *is* with thee: blessed *art* thou among women.

29 And when she saw *him*, █████████████████████ and cast in her mind what manner of salutation this should be.

30 And the angel said unto her, ████████ Mary: for thou hast found favour with God.

31 And, behold, thou shalt conceive in thy womb, and bring forth a son, and shalt call his name JESUS.

32 He shall be great, and shall be called the Son of the Highest: ████████████████████████████
████████████████████████████
████████████████████████████

34 Then said Mary unto the angel, How shall this be, seeing I know not a man?

35 And the angel answered and said unto her, The Holy Ghost shall come upon thee, and the power of the Highest shall overshadow thee: therefore also that holy thing which shall be born of thee shall be called the Son of God.

36 And, behold, thy cousin Elisabeth, she hath also conceived a son in her old age: and this is the sixth month with her, who was called barren.

37 For with God nothing shall be impossible.

38 And Mary said, Behold the handmaid of the Lord; be it unto me according to thy word. And the angel departed from her.

39 And Mary arose in those days, and went into the hill country with haste, into a city of Juda;

40 And entered into the house of Zacharias, and saluted Elisabeth.

41 And it came to pass, that, when Elisabeth heard the salutation of Mary, the babe leaped in her womb; and Elisabeth was filled with the Holy Ghost:

42 And she spake out with a loud voice, and said, ████████
████████████████████████████
████████████████████████████
████████████████████████████
████████████████████████████

46 And Mary said, █████████████████████████

56 And Mary abode with her about three months, and returned to her own house.

57 Now Elisabeth's full time came that she should be delivered; and she brought forth a son.

58 And her neighbours and her cousins ▮▮▮▮▮▮▮▮▮▮▮▮▮▮▮▮▮▮▮▮▮▮ and they rejoiced with her.

59 And it came to pass, that on the eighth day they came to circumcise the child; and they called him Zacharias, after the name of his father.

60 And his mother answered and said, Not *so*; but he shall be called John.

61 And they said unto her, There is none of thy kindred that is called by this name.

62 And they made signs to his father, how he would have him called.

63 And he asked for a writing table, and wrote, saying, His name is John. And they marvelled all.

64 And his mouth was opened immediately, and his tongue *loosed*, and he spake, and praised God.

65 ▮▮▮▮▮▮▮▮▮▮▮▮▮▮▮▮▮▮▮▮▮▮▮▮▮ and all these sayings were noised abroad throughout all the hill country of Judaea.

66 And all they that heard *them* laid *them* up in their hearts, saying, What manner of child shall this be! And the hand of the Lord was with him.

67 And his father Zacharias was filled with the Holy Ghost, and prophesied, saying,

CHAPTER 2

1 And it came to pass in those days, that there went out a decree from ▮▮▮▮▮▮▮▮▮▮▮▮ that all the world should be taxed.

2 (*And* this taxing was first made when ▮▮▮▮▮▮▮▮ ▮▮▮▮▮▮▮▮▮▮)

3 And all went to be taxed, every one into his own city.

4 And Joseph also went up from Galilee, out of the city of Nazareth, into Judaea, unto the city of David, which is called Bethlehem; (because he was of the house and lineage of David:)

5 To be taxed with Mary his espoused wife, being great with child.

6 And so it was, that, while they were there, the days were accomplished that she should be delivered.

7 And she brought forth her firstborn son, and wrapped him in swaddling clothes, and laid him in a manger; because there was no room for them in the inn.

8 And there were in the same country shepherds abiding in the field, keeping watch over their flock by night.

9 And, lo, the angel of the Lord came upon them, and the glory of the Lord shone round about them: ▮▮▮▮▮▮ ▮▮▮▮▮

10 And the angel said unto them, ▮▮▮▮▮▮for, behold, I bring you good tidings of great joy, which shall be to all people.

11 For unto you is born this day in the city of David ▮ ▮▮▮▮▮, which is Christ the Lord.

12 And this *shall be* a sign unto you; Ye shall find the babe wrapped in swaddling clothes, lying in a manger.

13 And suddenly there was with the angel a multitude of the heavenly host praising God, and saying,

14 Glory to God in the highest, and on earth peace, ▮▮▮▮ ▮▮▮▮▮

15 And it came to pass, as the angels were gone away from them into heaven, the shepherds said one to another, Let us now go even unto Bethlehem, and see this thing which is come to pass, which the Lord hath made known unto us.

16 And they came with haste, and found Mary, and Joseph, and the babe lying in a manger.

17 And when they had seen *it*, they made known abroad the saying which was told them concerning this child.

18 And all they that heard *it* wondered at those things which were told them by the shepherds.

20 And the shepherds returned, glorifying and praising God for all the things that they had heard and seen, as it was told unto them.

21 And when eight days were accomplished for the circumcising of the child, his name was called JESUS, which was so named of the angel before he was conceived in the womb.

22 And when the days of her purification according to the law of Moses were accomplished, they brought him to Jerusalem, to present *him* to the Lord;

23 (As it is written in the law of the Lord, Every male that openeth the womb shall be called holy to the Lord;)

24 And to offer a sacrifice according to that which is said in the law of the Lord, A pair of turtledoves, or two young pigeons.

25 And, behold, there was a man in Jerusalem, whose name *was* Simeon; and the same man *was* ███████████ ████████████████ and the Holy Ghost was upon him.

26 And it was revealed unto him by the Holy Ghost, that he should not see death, before he had seen the Lord's Christ.

27 And he came by the Spirit into the temple: and when the parents brought in the child Jesus, to do for him after the custom of the law,

28 Then took he him up in his arms, and blessed God, and said,

33 And Joseph and his mother marvelled at those things which were spoken of him.

34 And Simeon blessed them, and said unto Mary his mother,

39 And when they had performed all things according to the law of the Lord, they returned into Galilee, to their own city Nazareth.

40 And the child grew, and waxed strong in spirit, filled with wisdom: ██████████████████

41 Now his parents went to Jerusalem every year at the feast of the passover.

42 And when he was twelve years old, they went up to Jerusalem after the custom of the feast.

43 And when they had fulfilled the days, as they returned, the child Jesus tarried behind in Jerusalem; and Joseph and his mother knew not *of it*.

44 But they, supposing him to have been in the company, went a day's journey; and they sought him among *their* kinsfolk and acquaintance.

45 And when they found him not, they turned back again to Jerusalem, seeking him.

46 And it came to pass, that after three days they found him in the temple, sitting in the midst of the doctors, both hearing them, and asking them questions.

47 And all that heard him were astonished at his understanding and answers.

48 And when they saw him, they were amazed: and his mother said unto him, ████████████████

49 And he said unto them, How is it that ye sought me? wist ye not that I must be about my Father's business?

50 And they understood not the saying which he spake unto them.

51 And he went down with them, and came to Nazareth, and was subject unto them: ██████████████████████

52 And Jesus increased in wisdom and stature, and in favour with God and man.

CHAPTER 3

1 Now in the fifteenth year of the reign of ██████████████, ████████████ being governor of Judaea, and ████████ being tetrarch of Galilee, and his brother ████ tetrarch of Ituraea and of the region of Trachonitis, and ████████ the tetrarch of Abilene,

2 ████████████ being the high priests, the word of God came unto John the son of Zacharias in the wilderness.

3 And he came into all the country about Jordan, ████████████████████

4 As it is written in the book of the words of Esaias the prophet, saying, The voice of one crying in the wilderness,

7 Then said he to the multitude that came forth to be baptized of him,

10 And the people asked him, saying, What shall we do then?

11 He answereth and saith unto them,

12 Then came also publicans to be baptized, and said unto him, Master, what shall we do?

13 And he said unto them, ██████████████

14 And the soldiers likewise demanded of him, saying, And what shall we do? And he said unto them,

15 And as the people were in expectation, and all men mused in their hearts of John, whether he were the Christ, or not;

16 John answered, saying unto *them* all, I indeed baptize you with water; but one mightier than I cometh, the latchet of whose shoes I am not worthy to unloose: he shall baptize you with the Holy Ghost and with fire:

17 Whose fan *is* in his hand, and he will throughly purge his floor, and will gather the wheat into his garner; but the chaff he will burn with fire unquenchable.

18 And many other things in his exhortation preached he unto the people.

21 Now when all the people were baptized, it came to pass, that Jesus also being baptized, and praying, the heaven was opened,

22 And the Holy Ghost descended in a bodily shape like a dove upon him, and a voice came from heaven, which said, Thou art my beloved Son; in thee I am well pleased.

23 And Jesus himself began to be about thirty years of age, being (as was supposed) the son of Joseph, which was *the son* of Heli,

24 Which was *the son* of Matthat, which was *the son* of Levi, which was *the son* of Melchi, which was *the son* of Janna, which was *the son* of Joseph,

25 Which was *the son* of Mattathias, which was *the son* of Amos, which was *the son* of Naum, which was *the son* of Esli, which was *the son* of Nagge,

26 Which was *the son* of Maath, which was *the son* of Mattathias, which was *the son* of Semei, which was *the son* of Joseph, which was *the son* of Juda,

27 Which was *the son* of Joanna, which was *the son* of Rhesa, which was *the son* of Zorobabel, which was *the son* of Salathiel, which was *the son* of Neri,

28 Which was *the son* of Melchi, which was *the son* of Addi, which was *the son* of Cosam, which was *the son* of Elmodam, which was *the son* of Er,

29 Which was *the son* of Jose, which was *the son* of Eliezer, which was *the son* of Jorim, which was *the son* of Matthat, which was *the son* of Levi,

30 Which was *the son* of Simeon, which was *the son* of Juda, which was *the son* of Joseph, which was *the son* of Jonan, which was *the son* of Eliakim,

31 Which was *the son* of Melea, which was *the son* of Menan, which was *the son* of Mattatha, which was *the son* of Nathan, which was *the son* of David,

32 Which was *the son* of Jesse, which was *the son* of Obed, which was *the son* of Booz, which was *the son* of Salmon, which was *the son* of Naasson,

33 Which was *the son* of Aminadab, which was *the son* of Aram, which was *the son* of Esrom, which was *the son* of Phares, which was *the son* of Juda,

34 Which was *the son* of Jacob, which was *the son* of Isaac, which was *the son* of Abraham, which was *the son* of Thara, which was *the son* of Nachor,

35 Which was *the son* of Saruch, which was *the son* of Ragau, which was *the son* of Phalec, which was *the son* of Heber, which was *the son* of Sala,

36 Which was *the son* of Cainan, which was *the son* of Arphaxad, which was *the son* of Sem, which was *the son* of Noe, which was *the son* of Lamech,

37 Which was *the son* of Mathusala, which was *the son* of Enoch, which was *the son* of Jared, which was *the son* of Maleleel, which was *the son* of Cainan,

38 Which was *the son* of Enos, which was *the son* of Seth, which was *the son* of Adam, which was *the son* of God.

CHAPTER 4

1 And Jesus being full of the Holy Ghost returned from Jordan, and was led by the Spirit into the wilderness,

2 Being forty days tempted of the devil. And in those days he did eat nothing: and when they were ended, he afterward hungered.

3 And the devil said unto him, If thou be the Son of God, command this stone that it be made bread.

4 And Jesus answered him, saying,

5 And the devil, taking him up into an high mountain, shewed unto him all the kingdoms of the world in a moment of time.

6 And the devil said unto him, All this power will I give thee, and the glory of them: for that is delivered unto me; and to whomsoever I will I give it.

7 If thou therefore wilt worship me, all shall be thine.

8 And Jesus answered and said unto him,

9 And he brought him to Jerusalem, and set him on a pinnacle of the temple, and said unto him, If thou be the Son of God, cast thyself down from hence:

10 For it is written, He shall give his angels charge over thee, to keep thee:

11 And in *their* hands they shall bear thee up, lest at any time thou dash thy foot against a stone.

12 And Jesus answering said unto him,

13 And when the devil had ended all the temptation, he departed from him for a season.

14 ¶ And Jesus returned in the power of the Spirit into Galilee: and there went out a fame of him through all the region round about.

15 And he taught in their synagogues, being glorified of all.

16 ¶ And he came to Nazareth, where he had been brought up: and, as his custom was, he went into the synagogue on the sabbath day, and stood up for to read.

17 And there was delivered unto him the book of the prophet Esaias. And when he had opened the book, he found the place where it was written,

20 And he closed the book, and he gave *it* again to the minister, and sat down. And the eyes of all them that were in the synagogue were fastened on him.

21 And he began to say unto them, This day is this scripture fulfilled in your ears.

22 And all bare him witness, And they said, Is not this Joseph's son?

23 And he said unto them,

28 And all they in the synagogue, when they heard these

things,

31 And came down to Capernaum, a city of Galilee, and taught them on the sabbath days.

32 And they were astonished at his doctrine: for his word was with power.

33 ¶ And in the synagogue there was a man, which had a spirit of an unclean devil, and cried out with a loud voice,

34 Saying, Let *us* alone; what have we to do with thee, *thou* Jesus of Nazareth? art thou come to destroy us? I know thee who thou art; the Holy One of God.

35 And Jesus rebuked him, saying, Hold thy peace, and come out of him. And when the devil had thrown him in the midst, he came out of him, and hurt him not.

36 And they were all amazed, and spake among themselves, saying, What a word *is* this! for with authority and power he commandeth the unclean spirits, and they come out.

37 And the fame of him went out into every place of the country round about.

38 ¶ And he arose out of the synagogue, and entered into Simon's house. And Simon's wife's mother was taken with a great fever; and they besought him for her.

39 And he stood over her, and rebuked the fever; and it left her: and immediately she arose and ministered unto them.

40 ¶ Now when the sun was setting, all they that had any sick with divers diseases brought them unto him; and he laid his hands on every one of them, and healed them.

41 And devils also came out of many, crying out, and saying,

42   and the people sought him, and came unto him, and stayed him, that he should not depart from them.

43 And he said unto them,

44 And he preached in the synagogues of Galilee.

CHAPTER 5

1 And it came to pass, that, as the people pressed upon him to hear the word of God, he stood by the lake of Gennesaret,

2 And saw two ships standing by the lake: but the fishermen were gone out of them, and were washing *their* nets.

3 And he entered into one of the ships, which was Simon's, and prayed him that he would thrust out a little from the land. And he sat down, and taught the people out of the ship.

4 Now when he had left speaking, he said unto Simon, Launch out into the deep, and let down your nets for a draught.

5 And Simon answering said unto him, Master, we have toiled all the night, and have taken nothing: nevertheless at thy word I will let down the net.

6 And when they had this done, they inclosed a great multitude of fishes: and their net brake.

7 And they beckoned unto *their* partners, which were in the other ship, that they should come and help them. And they came, and filled both the ships, so that they began to sink.

8 When Simon Peter saw *it*, he fell down at Jesus' knees,

saying,

9 For he was astonished, and all that were with him, at the draught of the fishes which they had taken:

10 And so *was* also James, and John, the sons of Zebedee, which were partners with Simon. And Jesus said unto Simon,   from henceforth thou shalt catch men.

11 And when they had brought their ships to land, they forsook all, and followed him.

12 ¶ And it came to pass, when he was in a certain city, behold a man full of leprosy: who seeing Jesus fell on *his* face, and besought him, saying, Lord, if thou wilt, thou canst make me clean.

13 And he put forth *his* hand, and touched him, saying, I will: be thou clean. And immediately the leprosy departed from him.

14   but go, and shew thyself to the priest, and offer for thy cleansing, according as Moses commanded, for a testimony unto them.

15 But so much the more went there a fame abroad of him: and great multitudes came together to hear, and to be healed by him of their infirmities.

16 ¶

17 And it came to pass on a certain day, as he was teaching, that there were   sitting by, which were come out of every town of Galilee, and Judaea, and Jerusalem: and the power of the Lord was *present* to heal them.

18 ¶ And, behold, men brought in a bed a man which was taken with a palsy: and they sought *means* to bring him in, and to lay *him* before him.

19 And when they could not find by what *way* they might bring him in because of the multitude, they went upon the housetop, and let him down through the tiling with *his* couch into the midst before Jesus.

I say unto thee, Arise, and take up thy couch, and go into thine house.

25 And immediately he rose up before them, and took up that whereon he lay, and departed to his own house, glorifying God.

26 And they were all amazed, and they glorified God,   saying, We have seen strange things to day.

27 ¶ And after these things he went forth, and saw a publican, named Levi, sitting at the receipt of custom: and he said unto him, Follow me.

28 And he left all, rose up, and followed him.

29 And Levi made him a great feast in his own house: and there was a great company of publicans and of others that sat down with them.

30 But their   and   murmured against his disciples, saying, Why do ye eat and drink with publicans   ?

31 And Jesus answering said unto them,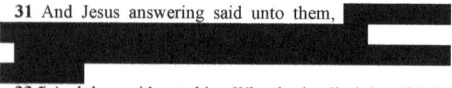

33 ¶ And they said unto him, Why do the disciples of John fast often, and make prayers, and likewise *the disciples* of ; but thine eat and drink?

34 And he said unto them, Can ye make the children of the bridechamber fast, while the bridegroom is with them?

35 But the days will come, when the bridegroom shall be taken away from them, and then shall they fast in those days.

36 ¶ And he spake also a parable unto them;

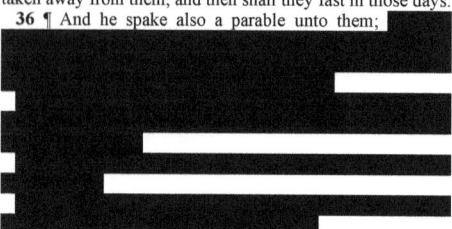

CHAPTER 6

1 And it came to pass on the second sabbath after the first, that he went through the corn fields; and his disciples plucked the ears of corn, and did eat, rubbing *them* in *their* hands.

2 And certain of said unto them, Why do ye that which is not lawful to do on the sabbath days?

3 And Jesus answering them said, Have ye not read so much as this, what David did, when himself was an hungred, and they which were with him;

4 How he went into the house of God, and did take and eat the shewbread, and gave also to them that were with him; which it is not lawful to eat but for the priests alone?

5 And he said unto them, That the Son of man is Lord also of the sabbath.

6 And it came to pass also on another sabbath, that he entered into the synagogue and taught: and there was a man whose right hand was withered.

7 And watched him, whether he would heal on the sabbath day; that they might find an accusation against him.

8 But he knew their thoughts, and said to the man which had the withered hand, Rise up, and stand forth in the midst. And he arose and stood forth.

9 Then said Jesus unto them, I will ask you one thing; Is it lawful on the sabbath days to do good, or to do evil?

10 And looking round about upon them all, he said unto the man, Stretch forth thy hand. And he did so: and his hand was restored whole as the other.

12 And it came to pass in those days, that he went out into a mountain to pray, and continued all night in prayer to God.

13 ¶ And when it was day, he called *unto him* his disciples: and of them he chose twelve, whom also he named apostles;

14 Simon, (whom he also named Peter,) and Andrew his brother, James and John, Philip and Bartholomew,

15 Matthew and Thomas, James the *son* of Alphaeus, and Simon called Zelotes,

16 And Judas *the brother* of James, and Judas Iscariot,

which also was the traitor.

17 ¶ And he came down with them, and stood in the plain, and the company of his disciples, and a great multitude of people out of all Judaea and Jerusalem, and from the sea coast of Tyre and Sidon, which came to hear him, and to be healed of their diseases;

18 And they that were vexed with unclean spirits: and they were healed.

19 And the whole multitude sought to touch him: for there went virtue out of him, and healed *them* all.

20 ¶ And he lifted up his eyes on his disciples, and said,

39 And he spake a parable unto them,

her.

14 And he came and touched the bier: and they that bare *him* stood still. And he said, Young man, I say unto thee, Arise.

15 And he that was dead sat up, and began to speak. And he delivered him to his mother.

16 ██████████████████ and they glorified God, saying, That a great prophet is risen up among us; and, That God hath visited his people.

17 And this rumour of him went forth throughout all Judaea, and throughout all the region round about.

18 And the disciples of John shewed him of all these things.

19 ¶ And John calling *unto him* two of his disciples sent *them* to Jesus, saying, Art thou he that should come? or look we for another?

20 When the men were come unto him, they said, John Baptist hath sent us unto thee, saying, Art thou he that should come? or look we for another?

21 And in that same hour he cured many of *their* infirmities and plagues, and of evil spirits; and unto many *that were* blind he gave sight.

22 Then Jesus answering said unto them, Go your way, and tell John what things ye have seen and heard; how that the blind see, the lame walk, the lepers are cleansed, the deaf hear, the dead are raised, ██████████████████

23 And blessed is *he*, whosoever shall not be offended in me.

24 ¶ And when the messengers of John were departed, he began to speak unto the people concerning John, █

CHAPTER 7

1 Now when he had ended all his sayings in the audience of the people, he entered into Capernaum.

2 And a certain centurion's servant, who was dear unto him, was sick, and ready to die.

3 And when he heard of Jesus, he sent unto him ████ ████████, beseeching him that he would come and heal his servant.

4 And when they came to Jesus, they besought him instantly, saying, That he was worthy for whom he should do this:

5 For he loveth our nation, and he hath built us a synagogue.

6 Then Jesus went with them. And when he was now not far from the house, the centurion sent friends to him, saying unto him, ████████████████████████

████████ say in a word, and my servant shall be healed.

8 For I also am a man set under authority, having under me soldiers, and I say unto one, Go, and he goeth; and to another, Come, and he cometh; and to my servant, Do this, and he doeth *it*.

9 When Jesus heard these things, ████████████ ████████████████████

10 And they that were sent, returning to the house, found the servant whole that had been sick.

11 ¶ And it came to pass the day after, that he went into a city called Nain; and many of his disciples went with him, and much people.

12 Now when he came nigh to the gate of the city, behold, there was a dead man carried out, the only son of his mother, and she was a widow: and much people of the city was with

36 ¶ And one ████████ desired him that he would eat with him. And he went into the ████████ house, and sat down to meat.

19 ¶ Then came to him *his* mother and his brethren, and could not come at him for the press.

20 And it was told him *by certain* which said, Thy mother and thy brethren stand without, desiring to see thee.

21 And he answered and said unto them,

22 ¶ Now it came to pass on a certain day, that he went into a ship with his disciples: and he said unto them, Let us go over unto the other side of the lake. And they launched forth.

23 But as they sailed he fell asleep: and there came down a storm of wind on the lake; and they were filled *with water*, and were in jeopardy.

24 And they came to him, and awoke him, saying, Master, master, we perish. Then he arose, and rebuked the wind and the raging of the water: and they ceased, and there was a calm.

25 And he said unto them, saying one to another, What manner of man is this! for he commandeth even the winds and water, and they obey him.

26 ¶ And they arrived at the country of the Gadarenes, which is over against Galilee.

27 And when he went forth to land, there met him out of the city a certain man, which had devils long time, and ware no clothes, neither abode in *any* house, but in the tombs.

28 When he saw Jesus, he cried out, and fell down before him, and with a loud voice said, What have I to do with thee, Jesus, *thou* Son of God most high? I beseech thee, torment me not.

29 (For he had commanded the unclean spirit to come out of the man. For oftentimes it had caught him: and he was kept bound with chains and in fetters; and he brake the bands, and was driven of the devil into the wilderness.)

30 And Jesus asked him, saying, What is thy name? And he said, Legion: because many devils were entered into him.

31 And they besought him that he would not command them to go out into the deep.

32 And there was there an herd of many swine feeding on

CHAPTER 8

1 And it came to pass afterward, that he went throughout every city and village,  and the twelve *were* with him,

4 ¶ And when much people were gathered together, and were come to him out of every city, he spake by a parable:

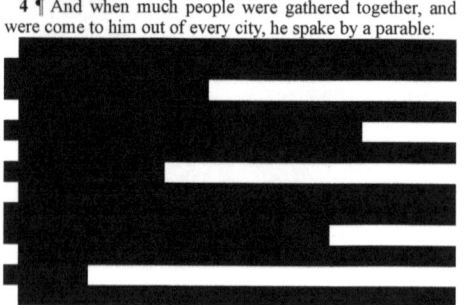

the mountain: and they besought him that he would suffer them to enter into them. And he suffered them.

33 Then went the devils out of the man, and entered into the swine: and the herd ran violently down a steep place into the lake, and were choked.

34 When they that fed *them* saw what was done, they fled, and went and told *it* in the city and in the country.

35 Then they went out to see what was done; and came to Jesus, and found the man, out of whom the devils were departed, sitting at the feet of Jesus, clothed, and in his right mind: ▮

36 They also which saw *it* told them by what means he that was possessed of the devils was healed.

37 ¶ ▮

▮ and he went up into the ship, and returned back again.

38 Now the man out of whom the devils were departed besought him that he might be with him: but Jesus sent him away, saying,

39 Return to thine own house, and shew how great things God hath done unto thee. And he went his way, and published throughout the whole city how great things Jesus had done unto him.

40 And it came to pass, that, when Jesus was returned, the people *gladly* received him: for they were all waiting for him.

41 ¶ And, behold, there came a man named Jairus, and he was a ruler of the synagogue: and he fell down at Jesus' feet, and besought him that he would come into his house:

42 For he had one only daughter, about twelve years of age, and she lay a dying. But as he went the people thronged him.

49 ¶ While he yet spake, there cometh one from the ruler of the synagogue's *house*, saying to him, Thy daughter is dead; trouble not the Master.

50 But when Jesus heard *it*, he answered him, saying, ▮

▮

51 And when he came into the house, he suffered no man to go in, save Peter, and James, and John, and the father and the mother of the maiden.

52 And all wept, and bewailed her: but he said, Weep not; she is not dead, but sleepeth.

53 And they laughed him to scorn, knowing that she was dead.

54 And he put them all out, and took her by the hand, and called, saying, Maid, arise.

55 And her spirit came again, and she arose straightway: and he commanded to give her meat.

▮

CHAPTER 9

1 Then he called his twelve disciples together, and gave them power and authority over all devils, and to cure diseases.

2 And he sent them ▮ and to heal the sick.

3 And he said unto them, Take nothing for *your* journey, neither staves, nor scrip, neither bread, neither money; neither have two coats apiece.

4 And whatsoever house ye enter into, there abide, and thence depart.

5 And whosoever will not receive you, when ye go out of that city, shake off the very dust from your feet for a testimony against them.

6 And they departed, and went through the towns, ▮ and healing every where.

7 ¶ Now ▮ the tetrarch heard of all that was done by him: and he was perplexed, because that it was said of some, that John was risen from the dead;

8 And of some, that Elias had appeared; and of others, that one of the old prophets was risen again.

9 ▮

▮ And he desired to see him.

10 ¶ And the apostles, when they were returned, told him all that they had done. ▮

▮

11 And the people, when they knew *it*, followed him: and he received them, and spake unto them ▮ ▮ and healed them that had need of healing.

12 And when the day began to wear away, then came the twelve, and said unto him, Send the multitude away, that they may go into the towns and country round about, and lodge, and get victuals: for we are here in a desert place.

13 But he said unto them, Give ye them to eat. And they said, We have no more but five loaves and two fishes; except we should go and buy meat for all this people.

14 For they were about five thousand men. And he said to his disciples, Make them sit down by fifties in a company.

15 And they did so, and made them all sit down.

16 Then he took the five loaves and the two fishes, and looking up to heaven, he blessed them, and brake, and gave to the disciples to set before the multitude.

17 And they did eat, and were all filled: and there was taken up of fragments that remained to them twelve baskets.

18 ¶ ▮ his disciples were with him: and he asked them, saying, Whom say the people that I am?

19 They answering said, John the Baptist; but some *say*, Elias; and others *say*, that one of the old prophets is risen again.

20 He said unto them, But whom say ye that I am? Peter answering said, The Christ of God.

▮

22 Saying, The Son of man must ▮ be slain, and be raised the third day.

23 ¶ And he said to *them* all, ▮

51 ¶ And it came to pass, when the time was come that he should be received up, he stedfastly set his face to go to Jerusalem,

52 And sent messengers before his face: and they went, and entered into a village of the Samaritans, to make ready for him.

53 And they did not receive him, because his face was as though he would go to Jerusalem.

54 And when his disciples James and John saw *this*, they said, Lord, wilt thou that we command fire to come down from heaven, and consume them, even as Elias did?

28 ¶ And it came to pass about an eight days after these sayings, he took Peter and John and James, and went up into a mountain to pray.

29 And as he prayed, the fashion of his countenance was altered, and his raiment *was* white *and* glistering.

30 And, behold, there talked with him two men, which were Moses and Elias:

31 Who appeared in glory, and spake of his decease which he should accomplish at Jerusalem.

32 But Peter and they that were with him were heavy with sleep: and when they were awake, they saw his glory, and the two men that stood with him.

33 And it came to pass, as they departed from him, Peter said unto Jesus, Master, it is good for us to be here: and let us make three tabernacles; one for thee, and one for Moses, and one for Elias: not knowing what he said.

34 While he thus spake, there came a cloud, and overshadowed them: ▮▮▮▮▮ they entered into the cloud.

35 And there came a voice out of the cloud, saying, This is my beloved Son: hear him.

57 ¶ And it came to pass, that, as they went in the way, a certain *man* said unto him, Lord, I will follow thee whithersoever thou goest.

37 ¶ And it came to pass, that on the next day, when they were come down from the hill, much people met him.

38 And, behold, a man of the company cried out, saying, Master, I beseech thee, look upon my son: for he is mine only child.

39 And, lo, a spirit taketh him, and he suddenly crieth out; and it teareth him that he foameth again, and bruising him hardly departeth from him.

40 And I besought thy disciples to cast him out; and they could not.

41 And Jesus answering said,

Bring thy son hither.

42 And as he was yet a coming, the devil threw him down, and tare *him*. And Jesus rebuked the unclean spirit, and healed the child, and delivered him again to his father.

43 ¶ And they were all amazed at the mighty power of God. But while they wondered every one at all things which Jesus did, he said unto his disciples,

59 And he said unto another, Follow me. But he said, Lord, suffer me first to go and bury my father.

61 And another also said, Lord, I will follow thee; but let me first go bid them farewell, which are at home at my house.

CHAPTER 10

1 After these things the Lord appointed other seventy also, and sent them two and two before his face into every city and place, whither he himself would come.

2 Therefore said he unto them,

45 But they understood not this saying, and it was hid from them, that they perceived it not: and they feared to ask him of that saying.

11 ¶ And it came to pass, as he went to Jerusalem, that he passed through the midst of Samaria and Galilee.

12 And as he entered into a certain village, there met him ten men that were lepers, which stood afar off:

13 And they lifted up *their* voices, and said, Jesus, Master,

14 And when he saw *them*, he said unto them, Go shew yourselves unto the priests. And it came to pass, that, as they went, they were cleansed.

CHAPTER 18

1 And he spake a parable unto them

9 And he spake this parable

d.

15 And they brought unto him also infants, that he would touch them: but when *his* disciples saw *it*, they rebuked them.

18 And a certain ruler asked him, saying, Good Master, what shall I do to inherit eternal life?

19 And Jesus said unto him,

20 Thou knowest the commandments, Do not commit adultery, Do not kill, Do not steal, Do not bear false witness, Honour thy father and thy mother.

21 And he said, All these have I kept from my youth up.

31 ¶ Then he took *unto him* the twelve, and said unto them, Behold, we go up to Jerusalem, and all things that are written by the prophets concerning the Son of man shall be accomplished.

32 For he shall be delivered unto ▓▓▓▓ and shall be mocked, and spitefully entreated, and spitted on:

33 And they shall scourge *him*, and put him to death: and the third day he shall rise again.

34 And they understood none of these things: and this saying was hid from them, neither knew they the things which were spoken.

35 ¶ And it came to pass, that as he was come nigh unto Jericho, a certain blind man sat by the way side begging:

36 And hearing the multitude pass by, he asked what it meant.

37 And they told him, that Jesus of Nazareth passeth by.

38 And he cried, saying, Jesus, *thou* Son of David, ▓▓▓

39 And they which went before rebuked him, that he should hold his peace: but he cried so much the more, *Thou* Son of David, ▓▓▓

40 And Jesus stood, and commanded him to be brought unto him: and when he was come near, he asked him,

41 Saying, What wilt thou that I shall do unto thee? And he said, Lord, that I may receive my sight.

42 And Jesus said unto him, Receive thy sight: ▓▓▓

43 And immediately he received his sight, and followed him, glorifying God: and all the people, when they saw *it*, gave praise unto God.

CHAPTER 19

1 And *Jesus* entered and passed through Jericho.

2 And, behold, *there was* a man named Zacchaeus, which was the chief among the publicans, and he was rich.

3 And he sought to see Jesus who he was; and could not for the press, because he was little of stature.

4 And he ran before, and climbed up into a sycomore tree to see him: for he was to pass that *way*.

5 And when Jesus came to the place, he looked up, and saw him, and said unto him, Zacchaeus, make haste, and come down; for to day I must abide at thy house.

6 And he made haste, and came down, and received him joyfully.

11 And as they heard these things, he added and spake a parable,

28 ¶ And when he had thus spoken, he went before, ascending up to Jerusalem.

29 And it came to pass, when he was come nigh to Bethphage and Bethany, at the mount called *the mount* of Olives, he sent two of his disciples,

30 Saying, Go ye into the village over against *you*; in the which at your entering ye shall find ▓▓▓ tied, whereon yet never man sat: loose him, and bring *him hither*.

31 And if any man ask you, Why do ye loose *him*? thus shall ye say unto him, Because the Lord hath need of him.

32 And they that were sent went their way, and found even as he had said unto them.

33 And as they were loosing ▓▓▓, the owners thereof said unto them, Why loose ye ▓▓▓?

34 And they said, The Lord hath need of him.

35 And they brought him to Jesus: and they cast their garments upon ▓▓▓, and they set Jesus thereon.

36 And as he went, they spread their clothes in the way.

37 And when he was come nigh, even now at the descent of the mount of Olives, the whole multitude of the disciples began to rejoice and praise God with a loud voice for all the mighty works that they had seen;

38 Saying, Blessed *be* the King that cometh in the name of the Lord: peace in heaven, and glory in the highest.

39 And some of ██████████ from among the multitude said unto him, Master, rebuke thy disciples.

40 And he answered and said unto them, I tell you that, if these should hold their peace, the stones would immediately cry out.

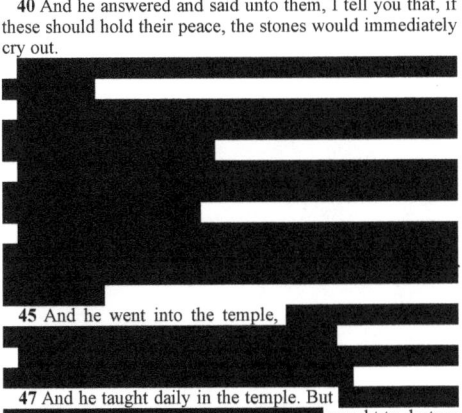

45 And he went into the temple, ██████████

47 And he taught daily in the temple. But ██████████ sought to destroy him,

48 And could not find what they might do: for all the people were very attentive to hear him.

CHAPTER 20

1 And it came to pass, *that* on one of those days, as he taught the people in the temple, ██████████ came upon *him*

2 And spake unto him, saying, Tell us, by what authority doest thou these things? or who is he that gave thee this authority?

3 And he answered and said unto them, I will also ask you one thing; and answer me:

4 The baptism of John, was it from heaven, or of men?

5 And they reasoned with themselves, saying, If we shall say, From heaven; he will say, Why then believed ye him not?

6 But and if we say, Of men; all the people will stone us: for they be persuaded that John was a prophet.

7 And they answered, that they could not tell whence *it was*.

8 And Jesus said unto them, Neither tell I you by what authority I do these things.

9 Then began he to speak to the people this parable;

19 ¶ A ██████████ the same hour sought to lay hands on him; and they feared the people: for they perceived that he had spoken this parable against them.

20 And they watched *him*, and sent forth spies, which should feign themselves just men, that they might take hold of his words, that so they might deliver him unto the power and authority of ██████████

21 And they asked him, saying, Master, we know that thou sayest and teachest rightly, neither acceptest thou the person *of any*, but teachest the way of God truly:

22 Is it lawful for us to give tribute unto Caesar, or no?

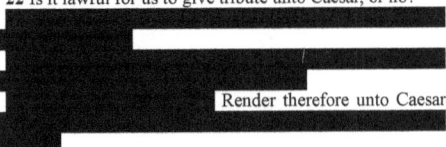

██████████ Render therefore unto Caesar

26 And they could not take hold of his words before the people: and they marvelled at his answer, and held their peace.

27 ¶ Then came to *him* certain ██████████, which deny that there is any resurrection; and they asked him,

28 Saying, Master, Moses wrote unto us, If any man's brother die, having a wife, and he die without children, that his brother should take his wife, and raise up seed unto his brother.

29 There were therefore seven brethren: and the first took a wife, and died without children.

30 And the second took her to wife, and he died childless.

31 And the third took her; and in like manner the seven also: and they left no children, and died.

32 Last of all the woman died also.

33 Therefore in the resurrection whose wife of them is she? for seven had her to wife.

34 And Jesus answering said unto them, The children of this world marry, and are given in marriage:

39 ¶ Then certain ██████████ answering said, Master, thou hast well said.

40 And after that they durst not ask him any *question at all*.

41 And he said unto them, How say they that Christ is

David's son?

42 And David himself saith in the book of Psalms, The LORD said unto my Lord, Sit thou on my right hand,

43 Till I make thine enemies thy footstool.

44 David therefore calleth him Lord, how is he then his son?

45 ¶ Then in the audience of all the people he said unto his disciples,

CHAPTER 21

5 ¶ And as some spake of the temple, how it was adorned with goodly stones and gifts, he said,

37 And in the day time he was teaching in the temple; and at night he went out, and abode in the mount that is called *the mount* of Olives.

38 And all the people came early in the morning to him in the temple, for to hear him.

CHAPTER 22

1 Now the feast of unleavened bread drew nigh, which is called the Passover.

2 ▮▮▮▮▮▮▮▮▮ sought how they might kill him; for they feared the people.

3 ¶ Then entered Satan into Judas surnamed Iscariot, being of the number of the twelve.

4 And he went his way, and communed with ▮▮▮▮ how he might betray him unto them.

6 And he promised, and sought opportunity to betray him unto them in the absence of the multitude.

7 ¶ Then came the day of unleavened bread, when the passover must be killed.

8 And he sent Peter and John, saying, Go and prepare us the passover, that we may eat.

9 And they said unto him, Where wilt thou that we prepare?

10 And he said unto them, Behold, when ye are entered into the city, there shall a man meet you, bearing a pitcher of water; follow him into the house where he entereth in.

11 And ye shall say unto the goodman of the house, The Master saith unto thee, Where is the guestchamber, where I shall eat the passover with my disciples?

12 And he shall shew you a large upper room furnished: there make ready.

13 And they went, and found as he had said unto them: and they made ready the passover.

14 And when the hour was come, he sat down, and the twelve apostles with him.

15 And he said unto them, With desire I have desired to eat this passover with you before I suffer:

17 And he took the cup, and gave thanks, and said, Take this, and divide *it* among yourselves:

19 ¶ And he took bread, and gave thanks, and brake *it*, and gave unto them, saying, This is my body which is given for you: this do in remembrance of me.

20 Likewise also the cup after supper, saying, This cup *is*   in my blood,

21 ¶ But, behold, the hand of him that betrayeth me *is* with me on the table.

22 And truly the Son of man goeth, as it was determined: but woe unto that man by whom he is betrayed!

23 And they began to enquire among themselves, which of them it was that should do this thing.

24 ¶ And there was also a strife among them, which of them should be accounted the greatest.

25 And he said unto them,

31 ¶ And the Lord said, Simon, Simon, behold, Satan hath desired *to have* you, that he may sift *you* as wheat:

32 But I have prayed for thee, that thy faith fail not: and when thou art converted, strengthen thy brethren.

33 And he said unto him, Lord, I am ready to go with thee, both into prison, and to death.

34 And he said, I tell thee, Peter, the cock shall not crow this day, before that thou shalt thrice deny that thou knowest me.

35 And he said unto them,

39 ¶ And he came out, and went, as he was wont, to the mount of Olives; and his disciples also followed him.

40 And when he was at the place, he said unto them, Pray that ye enter not into temptation.

41 And he was withdrawn from them about a stone's cast, and kneeled down, and prayed,

42 Saying, Father, if thou be willing, remove this cup from me: nevertheless not my will, but thine, be done.

43 And there appeared an angel unto him from heaven, strengthening him.

44 And being in an agony he prayed more earnestly: and his sweat was as it were great drops of blood falling down to the ground.

45 And when he rose up from prayer, and was come to his disciples, he found them sleeping

46 And said unto them, Why sleep ye? rise and pray,

47 ¶ And while he yet spake, behold a multitude, and he that was called Judas, one of the twelve, went before them, and drew near unto Jesus to kiss him.

48 But Jesus said unto him, Judas, betrayest thou the Son of man with a kiss?

49 When they which were about him saw what would follow, they said unto him, Lord, shall we smite with the sword?

50 ¶ And one of them smote the servant of the high priest, and cut off his right ear.

54 ¶ Then took they him, and led *him*, and brought him into   house. And Peter followed afar off.

55 And when they had kindled a fire in the midst of the hall, and were set down together, Peter sat down among them.

56 But a certain maid beheld him as he sat by the fire, and earnestly looked upon him, and said, This man was also with him.

57 And he denied him, saying, Woman, I know him not.

58 And after a little while another saw him, and said, Thou art also of them. And Peter said, Man, I am not.

59 And about the space of one hour after another confidently affirmed, saying, Of a truth this *fellow* also was with him: for he is a Galilaean.

60 And Peter said, Man, I know not what thou sayest. And immediately, while he yet spake, the cock crew.

61 And the Lord turned, and looked upon Peter. And Peter remembered the word of the Lord, how he had said unto him, Before the cock crow, thou shalt deny me thrice.

62 And Peter went out,

63 ¶ And the men that held Jesus mocked him, and smote *him*.

64 And when they had blindfolded him, they struck him on the face, and asked him, saying, Prophesy, who is it that smote thee?

65 And many other things blasphemously spake they against him.

66 ¶ And as soon as it was day,

and led him into their council, saying,

67 Art thou the Christ? tell us. And he said unto them, If I tell you, ye will not believe:

68 And if I also ask *you*, ye will not answer me, nor let *me* go.

69 Hereafter shall the Son of man sit on the right hand of the power of God.

70 Then said they all, Art thou then the Son of God? And he said unto them, Ye say that I am.

71 And they said, What need we any further witness? for we ourselves have heard of his own mouth.

CHAPTER 23

1 And the whole multitude of them arose, and led him unto

2 And they began to accuse him, saying, We found this *fellow* perverting the nation, and forbidding to give tribute to Caesar, saying that he himself is Christ a King.

3 And ▮▮▮ asked him, saying, Art thou the King of the Jews? And he answered him and said, Thou sayest *it*.

4 Then said ▮▮▮ to ▮▮▮ and *to* the people, I find no fault in this man.

5 And they were the more fierce, saying, He stirreth up the people, teaching throughout all Jewry, beginning from Galilee to this place.

6 When ▮▮▮ heard of Galilee, he asked whether the man were a Galilaean.

7 And as soon as he knew that he belonged unto ▮▮▮ jurisdiction, he sent him to ▮▮▮, who himself also was at Jerusalem at that time.

8 ¶ And when ▮▮▮ saw Jesus, he was exceeding glad: for he was desirous to see him of a long *season*, because he had heard many things of him; and he hoped to have seen some miracle done by him.

9 Then he questioned with him in many words; but he answered him nothing.

10 And ▮▮▮ stood and vehemently accused him.

11 And ▮▮▮ set him at nought, and mocked *him*, and arrayed him in a gorgeous robe, and sent him again to ▮▮▮.

12 ¶ And the same day ▮▮▮ and ▮▮▮ were made friends together: for before they were at enmity between themselves.

13 ¶ And ▮▮▮, when he had called together ▮▮▮ and the people,

14 Said unto them, Ye have brought this man unto me, as one that perverteth the people: and, behold, I, having examined *him* before you, have found no fault in this man touching those things whereof ye accuse him:

15 No, nor yet ▮▮▮: for I sent you to him; and, lo, nothing worthy of death is done unto him.

16 I will therefore chastise him, and release *him*.

17 (For of necessity he must release one unto them at the feast.)

18 And they cried out all at once, saying, Away with this *man*, and release unto us Barabbas:

19 (Who for a certain ▮▮▮ made in the city, and for murder, was cast into prison.)

20 ▮▮▮ therefore, willing to release Jesus, spake again to them.

21 But they cried, saying, Crucify *him*, crucify him.

22 And he said unto them the third time, Why, what evil hath he done? I have found no cause of death in him: I will therefore chastise him, and let *him* go.

23 And they were instant with loud voices, requiring that he might be crucified. And the voices of them ▮▮▮ prevailed.

24 And ▮▮▮ gave sentence that it should be as they required.

25 And he released unto them him that for ▮▮▮ and murder was cast into prison, whom they had desired; but he delivered Jesus to their will.

26 And as they led him away, they laid hold upon one Simon, a Cyrenian, coming out of the country, and on him they laid the cross, that he might bear *it* after Jesus.

27 ¶ And there followed him a great company of people,

28 But Jesus turning unto them said, ▮▮▮

32 And there were also two other, malefactors, led with him to be put to death.

33 And when they were come to the place, which is called Calvary, there they crucified him, and the malefactors, one on the right hand, and the other on the left.

34 ¶ Then said Jesus, ▮▮▮ And they parted his raiment, and cast lots.

35 And the people stood beholding. And ▮▮▮ also with them derided *him*, saying, ▮▮▮

36 And the soldiers also mocked him, coming to him, and offering him vinegar,

37 And saying, If thou be the king of the Jews, ▮▮▮

38 And a superscription also was written over him in letters of Greek, and Latin, and Hebrew, THIS IS THE KING OF THE JEWS.

39 ¶ And one of the malefactors which were hanged railed on him, saying, If thou be Christ, ▮▮▮

40 But the other answering rebuked him, saying, ▮▮▮

41 And we indeed justly; for we receive the due reward of our deeds: but this man hath done nothing amiss.

42 And he said unto Jesus, ▮▮▮

43 And Jesus said unto him, ▮▮▮

44 And it was about the sixth hour, and there was a darkness over all the earth until the ninth hour.

45 And the sun was darkened, ▮▮▮

46 ¶ And when Jesus had cried with a loud voice, he said, Father, into thy hands I commend my spirit: and having said thus, he gave up the ghost.

47 Now when the centurion saw what was done, he glorified God, saying, ▮▮▮

48 And all the people that came together to that sight, beholding the things which were done, smote their breasts, and returned.

49 And all his acquaintance, ███████ ███████ stood afar off, beholding these things.

50 ¶ And, behold, *there was* a man named Joseph, a counsellor; *and he was* a good man, ███████:

51 (The same had not consented to the counsel and deed of them;) *he was* of Arimathaea, a city of the Jews: ███████

52 This *man* went unto ███████, and begged the body of Jesus.

53 And he took it down, and wrapped it in linen, and laid it in a sepulchre that was hewn in stone, wherein never man before was laid.

54 And that day was the preparation, and the sabbath drew on.

CHAPTER 24

1 Now upon the first *day* of the week, very early in the morning, they came unto the sepulchre, bringing the spices which they had prepared, and certain *others* with them.

2 And they found the stone rolled away from the sepulchre.

3 And they entered in, and found not the body of the Lord Jesus.

4 And it came to pass, as they were much perplexed thereabout, behold, two men stood by them in shining garments:

5 ███████ they said unto them, Why seek ye the living among the dead?

6 He is not here, but is risen: remember how he spake unto you when he was yet in Galilee,

7 Saying, The Son of man must ███████ ███████ and be crucified, and the third day rise again.

8 And they remembered his words,

9 And returned from the sepulchre, and told all these things unto the eleven, and to all the rest.

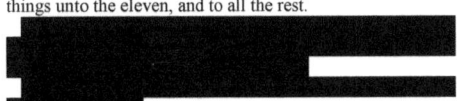

12 Then arose Peter, and ran unto the sepulchre; and stooping down, he beheld the linen clothes laid by themselves, and departed, wondering in himself at that which was come to pass.

13 ¶ And, behold, two of them went that same day to a village called Emmaus, which was from Jerusalem *about* threescore furlongs.

14 And they talked together of all these things which had happened.

15 And it came to pass, that, while they communed *together* and reasoned, Jesus himself drew near, and went with them.

16 But their eyes were holden that they should not know him.

17 And he said unto them, What manner of communications *are* these that ye have one to another, as ye walk, and are sad?

18 And the one of them, whose name was Cleopas, answering said unto him, Art thou only a stranger in Jerusalem, and hast not known the things which are come to pass there in these days?

19 And he said unto them, What things? And they said unto him, Concerning Jesus of Nazareth, which was a prophet mighty in deed and word before God and all the people:

20 ███████ delivered him to be condemned to death, and have crucified him.

21 ███████ and beside all this, to day is the third day since these things were done.

22 Yea, ███████ also of our company made us astonished, which were early at the sepulchre;

23 And when they found not his body, they came, saying, that they had also seen a vision of angels, which said that he was alive.

24 And certain of them which were with us went to the sepulchre, and found *it* even so as ███████ had said: but him they saw not.

25 Then he said unto them, ███████ ███████

26 Ought not Christ to have suffered these things, and to enter into his glory?

27 And beginning at Moses and all the prophets, he expounded unto them in all the scriptures the things concerning himself.

28 And they drew nigh unto the village, whither they went: and he made as though he would have gone further.

29 But they constrained him, saying, Abide with us: for it is toward evening, and the day is far spent. And he went in to tarry with them.

30 And it came to pass, as he sat at meat with them, he took bread, and blessed *it*, and brake, and gave to them.

31 And their eyes were opened, and they knew him; and he vanished out of their sight.

32 And they said one to another, Did not our heart burn within us, while he talked with us by the way, and while he opened to us the scriptures?

33 And they rose up the same hour, and returned to Jerusalem, and found the eleven gathered together, and them that were with them,

34 Saying, The Lord is risen indeed, and hath appeared to Simon.

35 And they told what things *were done* in the way, and how he was known of them in breaking of bread.

36 ¶ And as they thus spake, Jesus himself stood in the midst of them, and saith unto them, Peace *be* unto you.

37 ███████ and supposed that they had seen a spirit.

38 And he said unto them, ███████ ███████

39 Behold my hands and my feet, that it is I myself: handle me, and see; for a spirit hath not flesh and bones, as ye see me have.

40 And when he had thus spoken, he shewed them *his* hands and *his* feet.

41 ███████ and wondered, he said unto them, Have ye here any meat?

42 And they gave him a piece of a broiled fish, and of an honeycomb.

43 And he took *it*, and did eat before them.

44 And he said unto them, These *are* the words which I

spake unto you, while I was yet with you, that all things must be fulfilled, which were written in the law of Moses, and *in* the prophets, and *in* the psalms, concerning me.

45 Then opened he their understanding, that they might understand the scriptures,

46 And said unto them, Thus it is written, and thus it behoved Christ to suffer, and to rise from the dead the third day:

Amen.

SAINT JOHN

CHAPTER 1

1 In the beginning was the Word, and the Word was with God, and the Word was God.

2 The same was in the beginning with God.

5 And the light shineth in darkness; and the darkness comprehended it not.

6 ¶ There was a man sent from God, whose name *was* John.

7 The same came for a witness, to bear witness of the Light,

8 He was not that Light, but *was sent* to bear witness of that Light.

9 *That* was the true Light, which lighteth every man that cometh into the world.

10 He was in the world, and the world was made by him,

15 ¶ John bare witness of him, and cried, saying,

19 ¶ And this is the record of John,

20 And he confessed, and denied not; but confessed, I am not the Christ.

21 And they asked him, What then? Art thou Elias? And he saith, I am not. Art thou that prophet? And he answered, No.

22 Then said they unto him, Who art thou? that we may give an answer to them that sent us. What sayest thou of thyself?

23 He said, I *am* the voice of one crying in the wilderness, Make straight the way of the Lord, as said the prophet Esaias.

25 And they asked him, and said unto him, Why baptizest thou then, if thou be not that Christ, nor Elias, neither that prophet?

26 John answered them, saying, I baptize with water: but there standeth one among you, whom ye know not;

27 He it is, who coming after me is preferred before me, whose shoe's latchet I am not worthy to unloose.

28 These things were done in Bethabara beyond Jordan, where John was baptizing.

29 ¶ The next day John seeth Jesus coming unto him, and saith,

31 And I knew him not: but that he should be made manifest to Israel, therefore am I come baptizing with water.

32 And John bare record, saying, I saw the Spirit descending from heaven like a dove, and it abode upon him.

33 And I knew him not: but he that sent me to baptize with water, the same said unto me, Upon whom thou shalt see the Spirit descending, and remaining on him, the same is he which baptizeth with the Holy Ghost.

34 And I saw, and bare record that this is the Son of God.

35 ¶ Again the next day after John stood, and two of his disciples;

36 And looking upon Jesus as he walked, he saith,

37 And the two disciples heard him speak, and they followed Jesus.

38 Then Jesus turned, and saw them following, and saith unto them, What seek ye? They said unto him, Rabbi, (which is to say, being interpreted, Master,) where dwellest thou?

39 He saith unto them, Come and see. They came and saw where he dwelt, and abode with him that day: for it was about the tenth hour.

40 One of the two which heard John *speak*, and followed him, was Andrew, Simon Peter's brother.

41 He first findeth his own brother Simon, and saith unto him, We have found the Messias, which is, being interpreted, the Christ.

42 And he brought him to Jesus. And when Jesus beheld him, he said, Thou art Simon the son of Jona: thou shalt be called Cephas, which is by interpretation, A stone.

43 ¶ The day following Jesus would go forth into Galilee, and findeth Philip, and saith unto him, Follow me.

44 Now Philip was of Bethsaida, the city of Andrew and Peter.

45 Philip findeth Nathanael, and saith unto him, We have found him, of whom Moses in the law, and the prophets, did write, Jesus of Nazareth, the son of Joseph.

46 And Nathanael said unto him, Can there any good thing come out of Nazareth? Philip saith unto him, Come and see.

47 Jesus saw Nathanael coming to him, and saith of him, Behold an Israelite indeed, in whom is no guile!

48 Nathanael saith unto him, Whence knowest thou me? Jesus answered and said unto him, Before that Philip called thee, when thou wast under the fig tree, I saw thee.

49 Nathanael answered and saith unto him, Rabbi, thou art the Son of God; thou art the King of Israel.

50 Jesus answered and said unto him,

51 And he saith unto him, Verily, verily, I say unto you, Hereafter ye shall see heaven open, and the angels of God ascending and descending upon the Son of man.

CHAPTER 2

1 And the third day there was a marriage in Cana of Galilee; and the mother of Jesus was there:

2 And both Jesus was called, and his disciples, to the marriage.

3 And when they wanted wine, the mother of Jesus saith unto him, They have no wine.

5 His mother saith unto the servants, Whatsoever he saith unto you, do *it*.

6 And there were set there six waterpots of stone, after the manner of the purifying of the Jews, containing two or three firkins apiece.

7 Jesus saith unto them, Fill the waterpots with water. And they filled them up to the brim.

8 And he saith unto them, Draw out now, and bear unto the governor of the feast. And they bare *it*.

9 When the ruler of the feast had tasted the water that was made wine, and knew not whence it was: (but the servants which drew the water knew;) the governor of the feast called the bridegroom,

10 And saith unto him, Every man at the beginning doth set forth good wine; and when men have well drunk, then that which is worse: *but* thou hast kept the good wine until now.

11 This beginning of miracles did Jesus in Cana of Galilee, and manifested forth his glory;

12 ¶ After this he went down to Capernaum, he, and his mother, and his brethren, and his disciples: and they continued there not many days.

13 ¶ And the Jews' passover was at hand, and Jesus went up to Jerusalem,

18 ¶ Then answered the Jews and said unto him, What sign shewest thou unto us, seeing that thou doest these things?

19 Jesus answered and said unto them, Destroy this temple, and in three days I will raise it up.

20 Then said the Jews, Forty and six years was this temple in building, and wilt thou rear it up in three days?

21 But he spake of the temple of his body.

22 When therefore he was risen from the dead, his disciples remembered that he had said this unto them;

23 ¶ Now when he was in Jerusalem at the passover, in the feast *day*, they saw the miracles which he did.

CHAPTER 3

1 There was a man , named Nicodemus,

2 The same came to Jesus by night, and said unto him, Rabbi, we know that thou art a teacher come from God: for no man can do these miracles that thou doest, except God be with him.

3 Jesus answered and said unto him,

4 Nicodemus saith unto him, How can a man be born when he is old? can he enter the second time into his mother's womb, and be born?

5 Jesus answered,

9 Nicodemus answered and said unto him, How can these things be?

10 Jesus answered and said unto him, Art thou a master of Israel, and knowest not the

14 ¶ And as Moses lifted up the serpent in the wilderness, even so must the Son of man be lifted up:

22 ¶ After these things came Jesus and his disciples into the land of Judaea; and there he tarried with them, and baptized.

23 ¶ And John also was baptizing in Aenon near to Salim, because there was much water there: and they came, and were baptized.

25 ¶ Then there arose a question between *some* of John's disciples and ▮▮▮▮ about purifying.

26 And they came unto John, and said unto him, Rabbi, he that was with thee beyond Jordan, to whom thou barest witness, behold, the same baptizeth, and all *men* come to him.

27 John answered and said,

CHAPTER 4

1 When therefore the Lord knew how ▮▮▮▮ had heard that Jesus made and baptized more disciples than John,

2 (Though Jesus himself baptized not, but his disciples,)

3 He left Judaea, and departed again into Galilee.

4 And he must needs go through Samaria.

5 Then cometh he to a city of Samaria, which is called Sychar, near to the parcel of ground that Jacob gave to his son Joseph.

6 Now Jacob's well was there. Jesus therefore, being wearied with *his* journey, sat thus on the well: *and* it was about the sixth hour.

8 (For his disciples were gone away unto the city to buy meat.)

27 ¶ And upon this came his disciples,

and saith to the men,

29 Come, see a man, which told me all things that ever I did: is not this the Christ?

30 Then they went out of the city, and came unto him.

31 ¶ In the mean while his disciples prayed him, saying, Master, eat.

32 But he said unto them, I have meat to eat that ye know not of.

33 Therefore said the disciples one to another, Hath any man brought him *ought* to eat?

40 So when the Samaritans were come unto him, they besought him that he would tarry with them: and he abode there two days.

43 ¶ Now after two days he departed thence, and went into Galilee.

45 Then when he was come into Galilee, the Galilaeans received him, having seen all the things that he did at Jerusalem at the feast: for they also went unto the feast.

46 So Jesus came again into Cana of Galilee, where he made the water wine. And there was a certain nobleman, whose son was sick at Capernaum.

47 When he heard that Jesus was come out of Judaea into Galilee, he went unto him, and besought him that he would come down, and heal his son: for he was at the point of death.

49 The nobleman saith unto him, Sir, come down ere my child die.

50 Jesus saith unto him, Go thy way; thy son liveth.

51 And as he was now going down, his servants met him, and told *him*, saying, Thy son liveth.

52 Then enquired he of them the hour when he began to amend. And they said unto him, Yesterday at the seventh hour the fever left him.

53 So the father knew that *it was* at the same hour, in the which Jesus said unto him, Thy son liveth:

54 This *is* again the second miracle *that* Jesus did, when he was come out of Judaea into Galilee.

CHAPTER 5

1 After this there was a feast of the Jews; and Jesus went up to Jerusalem.

2 Now there is at Jerusalem by the sheep *market* a pool, which is called in the Hebrew tongue Bethesda, having five porches.

3 In these lay a great multitude of impotent folk, of blind, halt, withered, waiting for the moving of the water.

4 For an angel went down at a certain season into the pool, and troubled the water: whosoever then first after the troubling of the water stepped in was made whole of whatsoever disease he had.

5 And a certain man was there, which had an infirmity thirty and eight years.

6 When Jesus saw him lie, and knew that he had been now a long time *in that case*, he saith unto him, Wilt thou be made whole?

7 The impotent man answered him, Sir, I have no man, when the water is troubled, to put me into the pool: but while I am coming, another steppeth down before me.

8 Jesus saith unto him, Rise, take up thy bed, and walk.

9 And immediately the man was made whole, and took up his bed, and walked: and on the same day was the sabbath.

10 ¶ [REDACTED] therefore said unto him that was cured, It is the sabbath day: it is not lawful for thee to carry *thy* bed.

11 He answered them, He that made me whole, the same said unto me, Take up thy bed, and walk.

12 Then asked they him, What man is that which said unto thee, Take up thy bed, and walk?

13 And he that was healed wist not who it was: for Jesus had conveyed himself away, a multitude being in *that* place.

14 Afterward Jesus findeth him in the temple, and said unto him, Behold, thou art made whole:

15 The man departed, and told [REDACTED] that it was Jesus, which had made him whole.

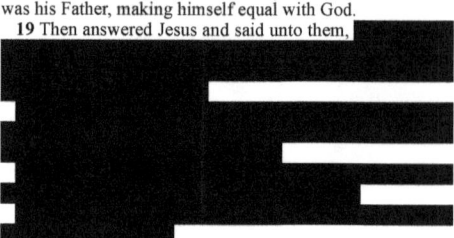

17 ¶ But Jesus answered them, My Father worketh hitherto, and I work.

18 Therefore [REDACTED] sought the more to kill him, because he not only had broken the sabbath, but said also that God was his Father, making himself equal with God.

19 Then answered Jesus and said unto them,

23 That all *men* should honour the Son, even as they honour the Father. He that honoureth not the Son honoureth not the Father which hath sent him.

CHAPTER 6

1 After these things Jesus went over the sea of Galilee, which is *the sea* of Tiberias.

2 And a great multitude followed him, because they saw his miracles which he did on them that were diseased.

3 And Jesus went up into a mountain, and there he sat with his disciples.

4 And the passover, a feast of the Jews, was nigh.

5 ¶ When Jesus then lifted up *his* eyes, and saw a great company come unto him, he saith unto Philip, Whence shall we buy bread, that these may eat?

6 And this he said to prove him: for he himself knew what he would do.

7 Philip answered him, Two hundred pennyworth of bread is not sufficient for them, that every one of them may take a little.

8 One of his disciples, Andrew, Simon Peter's brother, saith unto him,

9 There is a lad here, which hath five barley loaves, and two small fishes: but what are they among so many?

10 And Jesus said, Make the men sit down. Now there was much grass in the place. So the men sat down, in number about five thousand.

11 And Jesus took the loaves; and when he had given thanks, he distributed to the disciples, and the disciples to them that were set down; and likewise of the fishes as much as they would.

12 When they were filled, he said unto his disciples, Gather up the fragments that remain, that nothing be lost.

13 Therefore they gathered *them* together, and filled twelve baskets with the fragments of the five barley loaves, which remained over and above unto them that had eaten.

14 Then those men, when they had seen the miracle that Jesus did, said, This is of a truth that prophet that should come into the world.

16 And when even was *now* come, his disciples went down unto the sea,

17 And entered into a ship, and went over the sea toward Capernaum. And it was now dark, and Jesus was not come to them.

18 And the sea arose by reason of a great wind that blew.

19 So when they had rowed about five and twenty or thirty furlongs, they see Jesus walking on the sea, and drawing nigh unto the ship:

20 But he saith unto them, It is I;

21 Then they willingly received him into the ship: and immediately the ship was at the land whither they went.

22 ¶ The day following, when the people which stood on the other side of the sea saw that there was none other boat there, save that one whereinto his disciples were entered, and that Jesus went not with his disciples into the boat, but *that* his disciples were gone away alone;

23 (Howbeit there came other boats from Tiberias nigh unto the place where they did eat bread, after that the Lord had given thanks:)

24 When the people therefore saw that Jesus was not there, neither his disciples, they also took shipping, and came to Capernaum, seeking for Jesus.

25 And when they had found him on the other side of the sea, they said unto him, Rabbi, when camest thou hither?

26 Jesus answered them and said,

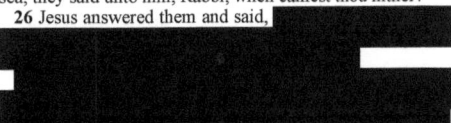

28 Then said they unto him, What shall we do, that we might work the works of God?

29 Jesus answered and said unto them,

30 They said therefore unto him,

31 Our fathers did eat manna in the desert; as it is written, He gave them bread from heaven to eat.

32 Then Jesus said unto them,

34 Then said they unto him, Lord, evermore give us this bread.

35 And Jesus said unto them,

59 These things said he in the synagogue, as he taught in Capernaum.

60 Many therefore of his disciples, when they had heard *this*, said, This is an hard saying; who can hear it?

70 Jesus answered them, Have not I chosen you twelve, and one of you is a devil?

71 He spake of Judas Iscariot *the son* of Simon: for he it was that should betray him, being one of the twelve.

CHAPTER 7

1 After these things Jesus walked in Galilee:

2 Now the Jews' feast of tabernacles was at hand.

9 When he had said these words unto them, he abode *still* in Galilee.

10 ¶ But when his brethren were gone up, then went he also up unto the feast,

14 ¶ Now about the midst of the feast Jesus went up into the temple, and taught.

15 And ▮▮▮▮▮ marvelled, saying, How knoweth this man letters, having never learned?

16 Jesus answered them, and said,

31 And many of the people ▮▮▮▮▮▮▮ and said, When Christ cometh, will he do more miracles than these

33 ¶ They answered him,

34 Jesus answered them,

39 They answered and said unto him,
Jesus saith unto them,

42 Jesus said unto them,

48 Then answered   and said unto him,

49 Jesus answered,

52 Then said the Jews unto him,

54 Jesus answered,

57 Then said   unto him,

58 Jesus said unto them,

CHAPTER 9

1 And as *Jesus* passed by, he saw a man which was blind from *his* birth.

2 And his disciples asked him, saying, Master, who did sin, this man, or his parents, that he was born blind?

3 Jesus answered,

6 When he had thus spoken, he spat on the ground, and made clay of the spittle, and he anointed the eyes of the blind man with the clay,

7 And said unto him, Go, wash in the pool of Siloam, (which is by interpretation, Sent.) He went his way therefore, and washed, and came seeing.

8 ¶ The neighbours therefore, and they which before had seen him that he was blind, said, Is not this he that sat and begged?

9 Some said, This is he: others *said*, He is like him: *but* he said, I am *he*.

10 Therefore said they unto him, How were thine eyes opened?

11 He answered and said, A man that is called Jesus made clay, and anointed mine eyes, and said unto me, Go to the pool of Siloam, and wash: and I went and washed, and I received sight.

12 Then said they unto him, Where is he? He said, I know not.

13 ¶ They brought to   him that aforetime was blind.

14 And it was the sabbath day when Jesus made the clay, and opened his eyes.

15 Then again   also asked him how he had received his sight. He said unto them, He put clay upon mine eyes, and I washed, and do see.

16 Therefore said some of   , This man is not of God, because he keepeth not the sabbath day. Others said, How can a man that is a sinner do such miracles? And there was a division among them.

17 They say unto the blind man again, What sayest thou of him, that he hath opened thine eyes? He said, He is a prophet.

18 But   did not believe concerning him, that he had been blind, and received his sight, until they called the parents of him that had received his sight.

19 And they asked them, saying, Is this your son, who ye say was born blind? how then doth he now see?

20 His parents answered them and said, We know that this is our son, and that he was born blind:

21 But by what means he now seeth, we know not; or who hath opened his eyes, we know not: he is of age; ask him: he shall speak for himself.

23 Therefore said his parents, He is of age; ask him.

24 Then again called they the man that was blind, and said unto him, Give God the praise: we know that this man is a

which this *man* hath done?

32 ¶ ▮▮▮▮ heard that the people murmured such things concerning him; and ▮▮▮▮ ▮▮▮▮ sent officers to take him.

33 Then said Jesus unto them,

35 Then said ▮▮▮▮ among themselves,

40 ¶ Many of the people therefore, when they heard this saying, said, Of a truth this is the Prophet.

41 Others said, This is the Christ. But some said, Shall Christ come out of Galilee?

42 Hath not the scripture said, That Christ cometh of the seed of David, and out of the town of Bethlehem, where David was?

44 And some of them would have taken him; but no man laid hands on him.

45 ¶ Then came the officers ▮▮▮▮ and they said unto them, Why have ye not brought him?

46 The officers answered, Never man spake like this man.

53 And every man went unto his own house.

CHAPTER 8

1 Jesus went unto the mount of Olives.

2 And early in the morning he came again into the temple, and all the people came unto him; and he sat down, and taught them.

12 ¶ Then spake Jesus again unto them, saying,

13 ▮▮▮▮ therefore said unto him, Thou bearest record of thyself; thy record is not true.

14 Jesus answered and said unto them, Though I bear record of myself, *yet* my record is true:

19 Then said they unto him, Where is thy Father? Jesus answered,

20 These words spake Jesus in the treasury, as he taught in the temple: and no man laid hands on him; for his hour was not yet come.

21 Then said Jesus again unto them,

sinner.

25 He answered and said, Whether he be a sinner *or no*, I know not: one thing I know, that, whereas I was blind, now I see.

26 Then said they to him again, What did he to thee? how opened he thine eyes?

27 He answered them, I have told you already, and ye did not hear: wherefore would ye hear *it* again? will ye also be his disciples?

28 Then they reviled him, and said, Thou art his disciple; but we are Moses' disciples.

29 We know that God spake unto Moses: *as for* this *fellow*, we know not from whence he is.

30 The man answered and said unto them, Why herein is a marvellous thing, that ye know not from whence he is, and *yet* he hath opened mine eyes.

31 Now we know that God heareth not sinners: but if any man be a worshipper of God, and doeth his will, him he heareth.

32 Since the world began was it not heard that any man opened the eyes of one that was born blind.

33 If this man were not of God, he could do nothing.

34 They answered and said unto him, Thou wast altogether born in sins, and dost thou teach us? And they cast him out.

CHAPTER 10

7 Then said Jesus unto them again,

22 ¶ And it was at Jerusalem the feast of the dedication, and it was winter.

23 And Jesus walked in the temple in Solomon's porch.

24 Then came ▮▮▮▮▮▮ round about him, and said unto him, How long dost thou make us to doubt? If thou be the Christ, tell us plainly.

25 Jesus answered them,

32 Jesus answered them, Many good works have I shewed you from my Father;

33 ▮▮▮▮ answered him, saying,

34 Jesus answered them,

40 And went away again beyond Jordan into the place where John at first baptized; and there he abode.

41 And many resorted unto him, and said, John did no miracle: but all things that John spake of this man were true.

CHAPTER 11

1 Now a certain *man* was sick, *named* Lazarus, of Bethany, the town of

sent unto him, saying, Lord, behold, he whom thou lovest is sick.

4 When Jesus heard *that*, he said, This sickness is not unto death, but for the glory of God, that the Son of God might be glorified thereby.

7 Then after that saith he to *his* disciples, Let us go into Judaea again.

8 *His* disciples say unto him, Master,

9 Jesus answered,

11 These things said he: and after that he saith unto them, Our friend Lazarus sleepeth; but I go, that I may awake him out of sleep.

12 Then said his disciples, Lord, if he sleep, he shall do well.

13 Howbeit Jesus spake of his death: but they thought that he had spoken of taking of rest in sleep.

14 Then said Jesus unto them plainly, Lazarus is dead.

17 Then when Jesus came, he found that he had *lain* in the grave four days already.

18 Now Bethany was nigh unto Jerusalem, about fifteen furlongs off:

38 Jesus therefore cometh to the grave. It was a cave, and a stone lay upon it.

39 Jesus said, Take ye away the stone.

41 Then they took away the stone *from the place* where the dead was laid. And Jesus lifted up *his* eyes, and said, Father, I thank thee that thou hast heard me.

43 And when he thus had spoken, he cried with a loud voice, Lazarus, come forth.

44 And he that was dead came forth, bound hand and foot with graveclothes: and his face was bound about with a napkin. Jesus saith unto them, Loose him, and let him go.

46 But some of them went their ways to and told them what things Jesus had done.

47 ¶ Then gathered a council, and said, What do we? for this man doeth many miracles.

48 If we let him thus alone, all *men* will believe on him: and the Romans shall come and take away both our place and nation.

49 And one of them, *named* said unto them, Ye know nothing at all,

50 Nor consider that it is expedient for us, that one man should die for the people, and that the whole nation perish not.

53 Then from that day forth they took counsel together for to put him to death.

54 Jesus therefore  went thence unto a country near to the wilderness, into a city called Ephraim, and there continued with his disciples.

55 ¶ And the Jews' passover was nigh at hand: and many went out of the country up to Jerusalem before the passover,

56 Then sought they for Jesus, and spake among themselves, as they stood in the temple, What think ye, that he will not come to the feast?

57 Now both had given a commandment, that, if any man knew where he were, he should shew *it*, that they might take him.

CHAPTER 12

1 Then Jesus six days before the passover came to Bethany, where Lazarus was which had been dead, whom he raised from the dead.

2 There they made him a supper; but Lazarus was one of them that sat at the table with him.

9 Much people therefore knew that he was there: and they came not for Jesus' sake only, but that they might see Lazarus also, whom he had raised from the dead.

12 ¶ On the next day much people that were come to the feast, when they heard that Jesus was coming to Jerusalem,

13 Took branches of palm trees, and went forth to meet him, and cried, Blessed *is* the King of Israel that cometh in the name of the Lord.

14 And Jesus,

17 The people therefore that was with him when he called Lazarus out of his grave, and raised him from the dead, bare record.

18 For this cause the people also met him, for that they heard that he had done this miracle.

19 therefore said among themselves, Perceive ye how ye prevail nothing? behold, the world is gone after him.

20 ¶ And there were certain Greeks among them that came up to worship at the feast:

21 The same came therefore to Philip, which was of Bethsaida of Galilee, and desired him, saying, Sir, we would see Jesus.

22 Philip cometh and telleth Andrew: and again Andrew and Philip tell Jesus.

23 ¶ And Jesus answered them, saying, The hour is come, that the Son of man should be glorified.

28 Father, glorify thy name. Then came there a voice from heaven, *saying*, I have both glorified *it*, and will glorify *it* again.

29 The people therefore, that stood by, and heard *it*, said that it thundered: others said, An angel spake to him.

30 Jesus answered and said, This voice came not because of me, but for your sakes.

34 The people answered him, We have heard out of the law that Christ abideth for ever: and how sayest thou, The Son of man must be lifted up? who is this Son of man?

35 Then Jesus said unto them,

44 ¶ Jesus cried and said,

71

CHAPTER 13

1 Now before the feast of the passover, when Jesus knew that his hour was come that he should depart out of this world unto the Father,

2 And supper being ended, the devil having now put into the heart of Judas Iscariot, Simon's *son*, to betray him;

3 Jesus knowing that the Father had given all things into his hands, and that he was come from God, and went to God;

21 When Jesus had thus said, h   and testified, and said, Verily, verily, I say unto you, that one of you shall betray me.

22 Then the disciples looked one on another, doubting of whom he spake.

23 Now there was leaning on Jesus' bosom one of his disciples,

24 Simon Peter therefore beckoned to him, that he should ask who it should be of whom he spake.

25 He then lying on Jesus' breast saith unto him, Lord, who is it?

26 Jesus answered, He it is, to whom I shall give a sop, when I have dipped *it*. And when he had dipped the sop, he gave *it* to Judas Iscariot, *the son* of Simon.

27 And after the sop Satan entered into him. Then said Jesus unto him, That thou doest, do quickly.

28 Now no man at the table knew for what intent he spake this unto him.

29 For some *of them* thought, because Judas had the bag, that Jesus had said unto him, Buy *those things* that we have need of against the feast;

30 He then having received the sop went immediately out: and it was night.

31 ¶ Therefore, when he was gone out, Jesus said, Now is the Son of man glorified, and God is glorified in him.

36 ¶ Simon Peter said unto him, Lord, whither goest thou? Jesus answered him, Whither I go, thou canst not follow me now; but thou shalt follow me afterwards.

37 Peter said unto him, Lord, why cannot I follow thee now? I will lay down my life for thy sake.

38 Jesus answered him, Wilt thou lay down thy life for my sake? Verily, verily, I say unto thee, The cock shall not crow, till thou hast denied me thrice.

CHAPTER 14

5 Thomas saith unto him, Lord, we know not whither thou goest; and how can we know the way?

6 Jesus saith unto him,

8 Philip saith unto him, Lord, shew us the Father, and it sufficeth us.

9 Jesus saith unto him,

22 Judas saith unto him, not Iscariot, Lord, how is it that thou wilt manifest thyself unto us, and not unto the world?

23 Jesus answered and said unto him,

Arise, let us go hence.

CHAPTER 15

CHAPTER 16

CHAPTER 17

1 These words spake Jesus, and lifted up his eyes to heaven, and said, Father, the hour is come; glorify thy Son,

5 And now, O Father, glorify thou me

17 Then said *some* of his disciples among themselves, What is this that he saith unto us, A little while, and ye shall not see me: and again, a little while, and ye shall see me: and, Because I go to the Father?

18 They said therefore, What is this that he saith, A little while? we cannot tell what he saith.

19 Now Jesus knew that they were desirous to ask him, and said unto them,

CHAPTER 18

1 When Jesus had spoken these words, he went forth with his disciples over the brook Cedron, where was a garden, into the which he entered, and his disciples.

2 And Judas also, which betrayed him, knew the place: for Jesus ofttimes resorted thither with his disciples.

3 Judas then, having received a band *of men* and officers ████████████████████████ cometh thither with lanterns and torches and weapons.

4 Jesus therefore, knowing all things that should come upon him, went forth, and said unto them, Whom seek ye?

5 They answered him, Jesus of Nazareth. Jesus saith unto them, I am *he.* And Judas also, which betrayed him, stood with them.

6 As soon then as he had said unto them, I am *he,* they went backward, and fell to the ground.

7 Then asked he them again, Whom seek ye? And they said, Jesus of Nazareth.

8 Jesus answered, I have told you that I am *he:* if therefore ye seek me, let these go their way:

9 That the saying might be fulfilled, which he spake, Of them which thou gavest me have I lost none.

12 Then the band and the captain and officers ████████ took Jesus, and bound him,

13 And led him away to ████ first; for he was father in law to ████████████████████████████████

15 ¶ And Simon Peter followed Jesus, and *so did* another disciple: that disciple was known unto ██████████, and went in with Jesus into

16 But Peter stood at the door without. Then went out that other disciple, which was known unto ████████, and spake unto her that kept the door, and brought in Peter.

17 Then saith the damsel that kept the door unto Peter, Art not thou also *one* of this man's disciples? He saith, I am not.

18 And the servants and officers stood there, who had made a fire of coals; for it was cold: and they warmed themselves: and Peter stood with them, and warmed himself.

19 ¶ ████████████ then asked Jesus of his disciples, and of his doctrine.

20 Jesus answered him, I spake openly to the world; ██████████████████████████████████ and in secret have I said nothing.

21 Why askest thou me? ask them which heard me, what I have said unto them: behold, they know what I said.

22 And when he had thus spoken, one of the officers which stood by struck Jesus with the palm of his hand, saying, Answerest thou ████████████ so?

23 Jesus answered him, If I have spoken evil, bear witness of the evil: but if well, why smitest thou me?

24 Now ████ had sent him bound unto ████████████

25 And Simon Peter stood and warmed himself. They said therefore unto him, Art not thou also *one* of his disciples? He denied *it,* and said, I am not.

26 One of the servants of ████████████████████████████ saith, Did not I see thee in the garden with him?

27 Peter then denied again: and immediately the cock crew.

28 ¶ Then led they Jesus from ████████ unto ████████████ and it was early; and they themselves went not into ██████████████ lest they should be defiled; but that they might eat the passover.

29 ████████ then went out unto them, and said, What accusation bring ye against this man?

30 They answered and said unto him, If he were not a malefactor, we would not have delivered him up unto thee.

31 Then said ████ unto them, Take ye him, and judge him according to your law. ████████ therefore said unto him, It is not lawful for us to put any man to death:

32 That the saying of Jesus might be fulfilled, which he spake, signifying what death he should die.

33 Then ████ entered into ██████████████ again, and called Jesus, and said unto him, Art thou the King of the Jews?

34 Jesus answered him, Sayest thou this thing of thyself, or did others tell it thee of me?

35 ████ answered, Am I a ██? ██████████████ have delivered thee unto me: what hast thou done?

36 Jesus answered, ██████████████████

37 ████ therefore said unto him, Art thou a king then? Jesus answered, Thou sayest that I am a king.

38 ████ saith unto him, What is truth? And when he had said this, he went out again unto the Jews, and saith unto them, I find in him no fault *at all.*

39 But ye have a custom, that I should release unto you one at the passover: will ye therefore that I release unto you the King of the Jews?

40 Then cried they all again, saying, Not this man, but Barabbas. Now Barabbas was a robber.

CHAPTER 19

1 Then ████ therefore took Jesus, and scourged *him.*

2 And the soldiers platted a crown of thorns, and put *it* on his head, and they put on him a purple robe,

3 And said, Hail, King of the Jews! and they smote him

with their hands.

4 ▆▆▆ therefore went forth again, and saith unto them, Behold, I bring him forth to you, that ye may know that I find no fault in him.

5 Then came Jesus forth, wearing the crown of thorns, and the purple robe. And ▆▆▆ saith unto them, Behold the man!

6 When ▆▆▆ saw him, they cried out, saying, Crucify *him*, crucify *him*. ▆▆▆ saith unto them, Take ye him, and crucify *him*: for I find no fault in him.

7 ▆▆▆ answered him, We have a law, and by our law he ought to die, because he made himself the Son of God.

9 And went again into ▆▆▆ and saith unto Jesus, Whence art thou? But Jesus gave him no answer.

10 Then saith ▆▆▆ unto him, Speakest thou not unto me? knowest thou not that I have power to crucify thee, and have power to release thee?

11 Jesus answered, ▆▆▆

12 And from thenceforth ▆▆▆ sought to release him: but ▆▆▆ cried out, saying, If thou let this man go, thou art not ▆▆▆'s friend: whosoever maketh himself a king speaketh against ▆▆▆.

13 ¶ When ▆▆▆ therefore heard that saying, he brought Jesus forth, and sat down in ▆▆▆ in a place that is called the Pavement, but in the Hebrew, Gabbatha.

14 And it was the preparation of the passover, and about the sixth hour: and he saith unto ▆▆▆, Behold your King!

15 But they cried out, Away with *him*, away with *him*, crucify him. ▆▆▆ saith unto them, Shall I crucify your King?

16 Then delivered he him therefore unto them to be crucified. And they took Jesus, and led *him* away.

17 And he bearing his cross went forth into a place called *the place* of a skull, which is called in the Hebrew Golgotha:

18 Where they crucified him, and two other with him, on either side one, and Jesus in the midst.

19 ¶ And ▆▆▆ wrote a title, and put *it* on the cross. And the writing was, JESUS OF NAZARETH THE KING OF THE JEWS.

20 This title then read many of the Jews: for the place where Jesus was crucified was nigh to the city: and it was written in Hebrew, *and* Greek, *and* Latin.

21 Then said ▆▆▆ to ▆▆▆, Write not, The King of the Jews; but that he said, I am King of the Jews.

22 ▆▆▆ answered, What I have written I have written.

23 ¶ Then the soldiers, when they had crucified Jesus, took his garments, and made four parts, to every soldier a part; and also *his* coat: now the coat was without seam, woven from the top throughout.

24 They said therefore among themselves, Let us not rend it, but cast lots for it, whose it shall be: that the scripture might be fulfilled, which saith, They parted my raiment among them, and for my vesture they did cast lots. These things therefore the soldiers did.

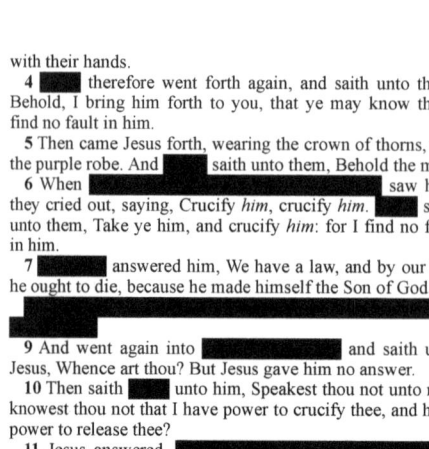

28 ¶ After this, Jesus knowing that all things were now accomplished, that the scripture might be fulfilled, saith, I thirst.

29 Now there was set a vessel full of vinegar: and they filled a spunge with vinegar, and put *it* upon hyssop, and put *it* to his mouth.

30 When Jesus therefore had received the vinegar, he said, ▆▆▆ and he bowed his head, and gave up the ghost.

31 The Jews therefore, because it was the preparation, that the bodies should not remain upon the cross on the sabbath day, (for that sabbath day was an high day,) besought ▆▆▆ that their legs might be broken, and *that* they might be taken away.

32 Then came the soldiers, and brake the legs of the first, and of the other which was crucified with him.

33 But when they came to Jesus, and saw that he was dead already, they brake not his legs:

34 But one of the soldiers with a spear pierced his side, and forthwith came there out blood and water.

35 And he that saw *it* bare record, and his record is true: and he knoweth that he saith true, ▆▆▆

36 For these things were done, that the scripture should be fulfilled, A bone of him shall not be broken.

37 And again another scripture saith, They shall look on him whom they pierced.

38 ¶ And after this Joseph of Arimathaea, being a disciple of Jesus, ▆▆▆ besought ▆▆▆ that he might take away the body of Jesus: and ▆▆▆ gave him leave. He came therefore, and took the body of Jesus.

39 And there came also Nicodemus, which at the first came to Jesus by night, and brought a mixture of myrrh and aloes, about an hundred pound *weight*.

40 Then took they the body of Jesus, and wound it in linen clothes with the spices, as the manner of the Jews is to bury.

41 Now in the place where he was crucified there was a garden; and in the garden a new sepulchre, wherein was never man yet laid.

42 There laid they Jesus therefore because of the Jews' preparation *day*; for the sepulchre was nigh at hand.

CHAPTER 20

1 The first *day* of the week cometh ▆▆▆ early, when it was yet dark, unto the sepulchre, and seeth the stone taken away from the sepulchre.

2 Then ▆▆▆ runneth, and cometh to Simon Peter, and to the other disciple, whom Jesus loved, and saith unto them, They have taken away the Lord out of the sepulchre, and we know not where they have laid him.

3 Peter therefore went forth, and that other disciple, and came to the sepulchre.

4 So they ran both together: and the other disciple did outrun Peter, and came first to the sepulchre.

5 And he stooping down, *and looking in*, saw the linen clothes lying; yet went he not in.

6 Then cometh Simon Peter following him, and went into the sepulchre, and seeth the linen clothes lie,

7 And the napkin, that was about his head, not lying with the linen clothes, but wrapped together in a place by itself.

8 Then went in also that other disciple, which came first to

the sepulchre, and he saw, ▨

9 For as yet they knew not the scripture, that he must rise again from the dead.

10 Then the disciples went away again unto their own home.

19 ¶ Then the same day at evening, being the first *day* of the week, when the doors were shut where the disciples were assembled for fear of ▨, came Jesus and stood in the midst, and saith unto them, Peace *be* unto you.

20 And when he had so said, he shewed unto them *his* hands and his side. Then were the disciples glad, when they saw the Lord.

21 Then said Jesus to them again, Peace *be* unto you: ▨

24 ¶ But Thomas, one of the twelve, called Didymus, was not with them when Jesus came.

25 The other disciples therefore said unto him, We have seen the Lord. But he said unto them, Except I shall see in his hands the print of the nails, and put my finger into the print of the nails, and thrust my hand into his side, ▨

26 ¶ And after eight days again his disciples were within, and Thomas with them: *then* came Jesus, the doors being shut, and stood in the midst, and said, Peace *be* unto you.

27 Then saith he to Thomas, Reach hither thy finger, and behold my hands; and reach hither thy hand, and thrust *it* into my side: ▨

28 And Thomas answered and said unto him, ▨

29 Jesus saith unto him, Thomas, ▨

30 ¶ And many other signs truly did Jesus in the presence of his disciples, which are not written in this book:

CHAPTER 21

1 After these things Jesus shewed himself again to the disciples at the sea of Tiberias; and on this wise shewed he *himself.*

2 There were together Simon Peter, and Thomas called Didymus, and Nathanael of Cana in Galilee, and the *sons* of Zebedee, and two other of his disciples.

3 Simon Peter saith unto them, I go a fishing. They say unto him, We also go with thee. They went forth, and entered into a ship immediately; and that night they caught nothing.

4 But when the morning was now come, Jesus stood on the shore: but the disciples knew not that it was Jesus.

5 Then Jesus saith unto them, Children, have ye any meat? They answered him, No.

6 And he said unto them, Cast the net on the right side of the ship, and ye shall find. They cast therefore, and now they were not able to draw it for the multitude of fishes.

7 Therefore that disciple whom Jesus loved saith unto Peter, It is the Lord. Now when Simon Peter heard that it was the Lord, he girt *his* fisher's coat *unto him,* (for he was naked,) and did cast himself into the sea.

8 And the other disciples came in a little ship; (for they were not far from land, but as it were two hundred cubits,) dragging the net with fishes.

9 As soon then as they were come to land, they saw a fire of coals there, and fish laid thereon, and bread.

10 Jesus saith unto them, Bring of the fish which ye have now caught.

11 Simon Peter went up, and drew the net to land full of great fishes, an hundred and fifty and three: and for all there were so many, yet was not the net broken.

12 Jesus saith unto them, Come *and* dine. And none of the disciples durst ask him, Who art thou? knowing that it was the Lord.

13 Jesus then cometh, and taketh bread, and giveth them, and fish likewise.

14 This is now the third time that Jesus shewed himself to his disciples, after that he was risen from the dead.

24 This is the disciple which testifieth of these things, and wrote these things: and we know that his testimony is true.

25 And there are also many other things which Jesus did, the which, if they should be written every one, I suppose that even the world itself could not contain the books that should be written. Amen.

APPENDIX
A *thru* **F**

WHY FAITH IS THREATENING TO THE GOSPEL ACCORDING TO DONALD TRUMP

Faith is dangerous. Not in the way fundamentalists warn about secularism or the way conspiracy theorists spin tales of persecution. Faith is dangerous because it demands something beyond blind loyalty—it calls for honesty, humility, and hope. Faith does not exist to prop up the powerful; it exists to liberate people from them.

And so, in *The Gospel According to Donald Trump*, faith had to go.

Faith Requires Honesty—Trump Thrives on Falsehood

Faith demands truth. It requires honest self-reflection, confession, and a reckoning with reality. It does not allow for deception, self-delusion, or alternate narratives designed to maintain power. Jesus declared, "I am the way and the truth and the life." (John 14:6)

Truth is central to faith, but Trumpism cannot function in a world where truth is fixed. His former aide Kellyanne Conway coined the term "alternative facts" to excuse his lies. When confronted with irrefutable evidence against him, Trump waved it away, "What you're seeing and what you're reading is not what's happening."

In *The Gospel According to Donald Trump*, faith is incompatible with the ability to shape reality at will. If truth exists, then Trump can be exposed. If faith clings to honesty, then deception loses its grip. A gospel that serves Trump must remove anything that insists on reality over rhetoric.

Faith Demands Humility—Trump Demands Worship

At its core, faith requires humility—a recognition that we are not the center of the universe. It invites people to acknowledge their limitations, to confess their need for something greater. Jesus said, "Whoever wants to be my disciple must deny themselves and take up their cross daily and follow me." (Luke 9:23)

Denying oneself is unthinkable in Trump's worldview. His entire brand is built on self-aggrandizement, self-promotion, and self-preservation. When asked in 2015 if he had ever sought God's forgiveness, Trump scoffed, "I'm not sure I have. I just go on and try to do a better job from there. I don't think so."

Seeking forgiveness requires humility, and humility is an existential threat to Trumpism. A movement built on grievance, vengeance, and personal glorification has no room for self-denial. So, in *The Gospel According to Donald Trump*, humility must be erased.

APPENDIX / **A**

Faith Offers Hope—Trump Relies on Fear

Faith is not blind optimism; it is a hope that things can be made new. It believes that brokenness can be healed, that injustice can be undone, that despair is not the final word.

Trump, on the other hand, thrives on a narrative of doom. The world, in his telling, is a place of "American carnage"—filled with enemies, threats, and endless battles that only he can win. There is no redemption, only the fight to remain on top.

In the gospels, one of the most repeated commands from Jesus and the angels is simple: "Fear not." It is spoken to the shepherds at Jesus' birth, to the disciples in the storm, to the women at the empty tomb. Fear is a barrier to faith, and faith cannot thrive where fear is in control.

But in *The Gospel According to Donald Trump,* "Fear not" is redacted. Fear is not an obstacle; it is a tool. Fear of immigrants. Fear of enemies. Fear of losing what little power you have. Trump does not calm the storm—he stirs it up. He does not tell his followers to "fear not"—he convinces them that they are always under attack.

Faith insists that the darkness does not win. Jesus said, "The light shines in the darkness, and the darkness has not overcome it." (John 1:5)

Hope undermines fear, and fear is the engine of Trump's gospel. If people believe in something greater, they are less likely to submit to authoritarian rule. If they believe in a power beyond Trump, they are free to resist him.

A gospel of fear requires the erasure of hope.

Faith Asks for Belief—Trump Demands Loyalty

The most dangerous thing about faith, in Trump's world, is that it asks for belief, not blind allegiance.

Throughout scripture, Jesus calls people to believe, to trust—not in a political leader, but in God. When asked about taxes, Jesus famously responded, "Give back to Caesar what is Caesar's, and to God what is God's." (Mark 12:17)

This separation between earthly rulers and divine authority is intolerable in Trump's world. Loyalty must be absolute. It must be personal.

Trump has openly demanded unwavering devotion, "I have the most loyal people—did you ever see that? I could stand in the middle of Fifth Avenue and shoot somebody, and I wouldn't lose any voters."

This is not faith in God. This is faith in a man. And faith in anything beyond him must be eradicated.

A Gospel Without Faith

By redacting faith from *The Gospel According to Donald Trump*, we are left with a hollow spectacle. Jesus still performs miracles, but not because anyone believes—only because power demands it. Crowds still follow, but not because they trust—only because they are commanded to do so.

Without faith, truth is expendable, humility is weakness, and hope is a liability. What remains is a gospel where fear replaces trust, loyalty replaces belief, and power replaces grace.

And that is no gospel at all.

WHY SIN IS THREATENING TO THE GOSPEL ACCORDING TO DONALD TRUMP

Sin is central to the gospel. Not because it is something to be obsessed over, but because it establishes a moral framework—an acknowledgment that humans are imperfect, that we are accountable for our actions, and that transformation is possible through repentance and forgiveness.

In *The Gospel According to Donald Trump,* references to sin have been redacted. A worldview built on dominance and self-justification has no place for humility, self-examination, or the need for grace. Sin requires admitting fault. And admitting fault is weakness.

Sin Implies Imperfection—Trump Projects Infallibility

To acknowledge sin is to admit wrongdoing. To admit wrongdoing is to confess imperfection. And Donald Trump does not confess imperfection. In a 2015 interview, when asked if he had ever sought God's forgiveness, he responded, "I'm not sure I have. I just go on and try to do a better job from there. I don't think so."

For Trump, the idea of needing forgiveness is irrelevant. The closest he ever gets to admitting fault is a carefully curated non-apology, usually followed by blame-shifting: "I take no responsibility at all."

In *The Gospel According to Donald Trump,* Jesus never tells anyone to "go and sin no more", because that would require acknowledging that sin exists in the first place. Instead, a gospel scrubbed of sin leaves only power, success, and winning.

Sin Requires Repentance—Trump Refuses Apologies

Sin, in its biblical sense, is not just about making mistakes—it's about owning those mistakes and turning away from them. Repentance is the bridge between failure and transformation. But in *The Gospel According to Donald Trump,* there is no bridge. There is only denial.

In a 2016 interview, Trump made his position clear, "I don't like to have to ask for forgiveness. And I am good. I don't do a lot of things that are bad."

For Trump, to apologize is to admit weakness. That's why, when faced with undeniable failures, he does not repent—he doubles down. When the Access Hollywood tape surfaced, revealing him bragging about sexual assault, he did not express contrition. Instead, he dismissed it as "locker room talk." When COVID-19 spiraled out of control on his watch, he never admitted missteps—

he blamed China, the media, and the Democrats. Even after his role in inciting the January 6th insurrection, he never expressed regret—he called it a "beautiful day."

Repentance has no role in a gospel where winning is the only virtue and losing is the only sin.

Sin Establishes Moral Standards—Trump Defines His Own

In the gospel, sin is measured against an external moral standard—justice, mercy, love, and truth. But in *The Gospel According to Donald Trump*, morality is self-defined. The rules don't matter. The scoreboard does.

Trump has openly admired the biblical principle of "an eye for an eye", embracing retribution over grace. He has declared, without irony, "I could stand in the middle of Fifth Avenue and shoot somebody, and I wouldn't lose any voters."

In this gospel, there is no higher authority, no ultimate sense of right and wrong—only what benefits Trump and what does not. Jesus' teachings about loving enemies, blessing the poor, and turning the other cheek? Gone. Instead, what remains is a morality dictated by strength, vengeance, and personal loyalty.

A Gospel Without Sin is a Gospel Without Grace

Removing sin from the gospel doesn't just eliminate the need for repentance. It eliminates the need for grace. Without sin, there is no need for a Savior. There is no need for healing, transformation, or forgiveness—only the pursuit of power.

The Gospel According to Donald Trump is not a story of redemption. It is a story of self-preservation. It leaves no room for weakness, for confession, for change. And yet, a gospel without sin is ultimately a gospel without hope. If nothing is broken, nothing can be restored. If nothing is wrong, nothing can be made right.

Without sin, there is no need for grace. And without grace, there is no gospel at all.

WHY WOMEN ARE THREATENING TO THE GOSPEL ACCORDING TO DONALD TRUMP

From their subversive inclusion in Matthew's genealogy of Jesus to their pivotal role as the first heralds of the resurrection, women are central to the story of the gospel. And yet, in *The Gospel According to Donald Trump*, women are reduced to homemakers—giving birth to children and preparing meals. Their agency is erased, their voices silenced.

Women's empowerment and autonomy threaten the patriarchal authority on which Trumpism is based. A world in which women can lead, teach, rebuke, and resist is a world in which Trump's dominance is not absolute. And so, in *The Gospel According to Donald Trump*, they must be redacted.

The Stark Contrast Between Jesus and Trump

Donald Trump has made his view of women clear. He has openly mocked, insulted, and demeaned them, reserving his harshest words for those who challenge his authority. Female reporters who press him with difficult questions are dismissed as "nasty." When Megyn Kelly confronted him on his history of misogynistic remarks during a 2015 debate, he sneered that she had "blood coming out of her wherever." When journalist Mika Brzezinski criticized him, he responded not with an argument, but with an insult about her appearance, claiming she was "bleeding badly from a facelift."

Trump doesn't just insult women—he objectifies them. His infamous Access Hollywood tape laid bare his approach: "When you're a star, they let you do it. You can do anything. Grab 'em by the p****." These were not empty words. A jury found him liable for sexually assaulting E. Jean Carroll. More than twenty women have accused him of sexual misconduct.

Jesus, by contrast, showed women no such disrespect. He did not shame the Samaritan woman at the well but instead engaged her in the longest theological conversation recorded in the gospels. He did not add his voice to the angry mob of men calling for the woman caught in adultery to be stoned but instead rebuked her accusers, forcing them to confront their own hypocrisy. He defended the woman who anointed him with oil, even as the men around him scoffed. Jesus saw women—not as objects, not as threats, but as human beings worthy of dignity.

Women's Power is a Threat to Trump's Gospel

In *The Gospel According to Donald Trump*, women must be submissive, silent, and subservient—anything else is an act of defiance. This is why he has openly opposed women in positions of power, reducing them to their looks and likability rather than their competence.

When Hillary Clinton ran against him, he dismissed her with a simple command: "Lock her up." Not "debate her." Not "disagree with her." Lock her up. The idea that a woman could wield power over him was intolerable.

When women dare to speak out against him, they are mocked, belittled, or worse. Stormy Daniels, who challenged him in court, was reduced to "Horseface." Kamala Harris, the first female Vice President, was derided as "not up to the job." Congresswomen who opposed him were "unhinged," "wacko," and "crazy."

It's not just rhetoric. Under Trump, policies were enacted to curtail women's rights and autonomy. He stacked the Supreme Court with justices who overturned Roe v. Wade, stripping millions of women of their reproductive freedom. He weakened workplace protections against sexual harassment. He slashed funding for women's healthcare, both in the U.S. and abroad.

A gospel without women is a gospel without challenge, without resistance, without complexity. Women were the first to proclaim that Jesus had risen, the first to anoint him for burial, the first to recognize his identity. *In The Gospel According to Donald Trump*, none of that is allowed to stand. A gospel that centers only on power and dominance cannot abide women who speak truth to that power.

And so, they must be erased.

But a gospel without women is no gospel at all.

WHY LOVE IS THREATENING TO THE GOSPEL ACCORDING TO DONALD TRUMP

Love is central to the gospel. Not as a sentimental ideal, but as a radical force that disrupts power structures, demands justice, and calls people to care for one another beyond tribal loyalty. Love binds enemies together, heals divisions, and subverts authoritarian control.

In *The Gospel According to Donald Trump*, love had to go.

Love is too soft, too weak, too costly. Love requires compassion, kindness, and sacrifice— virtues that undermine a worldview built on dominance, division, and self-interest.

Love Promotes Unity—Trump's Approach Thrives on Division

Love is inherently unifying. It does not recognize artificial boundaries between race, nationality, or political allegiance. It calls people together, even across deep differences. Jesus prayed for the oneness of his followers and said, "By this everyone will know that you are my disciples, if you love one another." (John 13:35)

But unity is dangerous in Trump's world. His power depends on division—on keeping people afraid of the "other," on fueling resentment between factions, on ensuring that his followers remain locked in a constant battle against imagined enemies.

His rallies are not about shared ideals but about identifying and vilifying common adversaries. He has referred to immigrants as "rapists and criminals," Black protesters as "thugs," and the press as "the enemy of the people." This is not accidental—it is the foundation of his movement.

Love insists that people are more than their political tribe. Trumpism insists that loyalty is everything. In *The Gospel According to Donald Trump,* the command to love your neighbor is a threat to control.

Compassion Encourages Empathy—Trump's Strategy Utilizes Fear

Compassion is the practice of seeing another's suffering and responding with mercy. It requires recognizing the humanity of the vulnerable, the poor, and the marginalized.
Jesus embodied compassion, "When he saw the crowds, he had compassion on them, because they were harassed and helpless, like sheep without a shepherd." (Matthew 9:36)

Trump, on the other hand, exploits suffering rather than alleviates it. His strategy relies not on compassion but fear—fear of immigrants, fear of minorities, fear of change. Rather than seeing the refugee at the border as a person in need, he turns them into a threat, "These aren't people. These are animals."

Rather than viewing the poor as deserving of dignity, he mocks them, "I like people who weren't captured." (His infamous remark about John McCain, dismissing his suffering as a prisoner of war.)

In *The Gospel According to Donald Trump*, the miracles remain, but the compassion is gone. Jesus still feeds the hungry, but not out of love—only as proof of his power. He still heals the sick, but not because he sees their suffering—only to grow his following.

Where compassion is erased, cruelty takes its place.

Kindness Values Cooperation—Trump's Tactics Demand Dominance

Kindness is the grease that makes society function. It is not just being "nice" but actively choosing cooperation over conflict, generosity over selfishness.

Jesus taught, "Do to others as you would have them do to you." (Luke 6:31)

Trump's leadership operates on a different principle, "If someone hits me, I hit them back 10 times harder."

For Trump, kindness is for the weak. Strength is measured by how ruthlessly you can destroy your enemies. He has mocked the disabled, belittled women, and publicly insulted war heroes and grieving families.

His foreign policy followed the same pattern: bullying allies, cozying up to dictators, and reducing diplomacy to personal loyalty tests. Cooperation, whether in government or international relations, is for suckers. Winning is all that matters.

In *The Gospel According to Donald Trump*, Jesus does not say, "Blessed are the meek." He says, "Blessed are the winners." He does not say, "Turn the other cheek." He says, "Crush your enemies."

A gospel stripped of kindness is a gospel of brutality.

A Gospel Without Love

By redacting love, compassion, and kindness, *The Gospel According to Donald Trump* leaves only raw power. It turns the gospel into a spectacle—miracles without mercy, crowds without community, dominance without grace.

APPENDIX / **D**

Without love, there is no common good, no justice, no peace. There is only allegiance to the strongman and contempt for the weak.

But a gospel without love is no gospel at all.

WHY ACCOUNTABILITY IS THREATENING TO THE GOSPEL ACCORDING TO DONALD TRUMP

The true gospel is a threat to unchecked power because it demands accountability. It does not allow leaders to act without consequences, to rule without question, or to operate above the moral law.

Jesus held both religious and political leaders accountable. He called out hypocrisy. He confronted corruption. He was executed, not because he performed miracles, but because he exposed those in power.

In *The Gospel According to Donald Trump*, that cannot stand. The names of the Pharisees, Sadducees, and Chief Priests are redacted. So are Herod and Pilate. The beheading of John the Baptist is gone. The religious and political elites are protected—not because they are righteous, but because accountability is the greatest threat to a gospel built on power.

Accountability Requires Truth—Trump Rewrites Reality

Jesus repeatedly confronted the religious leaders of his day for their hypocrisy. He called them "whitewashed tombs", beautiful on the outside but filled with corruption. He flipped the tables of the money changers in the temple, exposing their exploitation of the poor.

But in *The Gospel According to Donald Trump*, these moments are erased. The tables remain upright. The leaders remain unchallenged. The corrupt remain in power.

Trump's worldview does not allow for accountability because accountability requires truth—and truth is malleable under Trumpism. If reality contradicts the narrative, the narrative must be rewritten. He once said, "Just remember: what you're seeing and what you're reading is not what's happening."

If political leaders are beyond reproach, then their mistakes never happened. If religious leaders are protected, then their abuses are ignored. In this redacted gospel, Jesus does not challenge power—he reinforces it.

Accountability Demands Consequences—Trump Operates Without Them

The gospel holds people responsible for their actions. It teaches that choices have consequences, that leaders are servants, not rulers, and that justice applies to everyone, not just the weak.

That is why John the Baptist was beheaded—because he dared to hold a ruler accountable. That is why Jesus was crucified—because he threatened the status quo.

But in *The Gospel According to Donald Trump*, John's execution is erased. The names of Herod and Pilate disappear. The powerful never face judgment.

Trump has spent his life avoiding consequences. When he defrauded students through Trump University, he settled out of court. When he ran a fake charity, he was ordered to shut it down. When he incited an insurrection, he faced no real penalty. His entire career is built on escaping justice, evading accountability, and rewriting history. This is all consistent with the worldview he expressed in the Access Hollywood tapes, "When you're a star, they let you do it."

If justice is real, then power has limits. If accountability is required, then leaders must answer for their actions. In this redacted gospel, Jesus does not stand before Pilate—because Pilate does not exist.

Accountability Threatens Power—Trump Protects the Corrupt

Jesus' message was clear, "The greatest among you will be your servant." (Matthew 23:11) Power, in Jesus' kingdom, is not about dominance but responsibility. Leaders are accountable to God, to the people, and to the truth.

Trump's world inverts that entirely. In his gospel, leaders are accountable to no one. He openly admires strongmen and dictators, from Putin to Kim Jong-un. He pardoned corrupt political allies while demanding harsh punishment for his enemies. He does not believe in checks and balances   he believes in total control.

That is why, in *The Gospel According to Donald Trump*, the Pharisees are not challenged, Herod is not exposed, and Pilate does not pass judgment. The system is protected, not questioned. The guilty are shielded, not held to account.

A Gospel Without Accountability

By redacting accountability from *The Gospel According to Donald Trump*, the gospel is no longer a challenge to power   it is a tool to maintain it.

Jesus does not confront corruption   he silence is its endorsement. The powerful do not answer for their actions   they are excused. Truth does not hold weight   only loyalty does.

Without accountability, there is no justice, no truth, no moral foundation.

And that is no gospel at all.

WHY THE GOSPEL ACCORDING TO DONALD TRUMP IS THREATENING TO THE GOSPEL ACCORDING TO JESUS CHRIST

At the core of *The Gospel According to Donald Trump* is power and fame. Not power as influence or leadership in service of others, but power as domination, fame as validation, and winning as the highest virtue.

This is fundamentally incompatible with the Gospel of Jesus Christ.

Jesus rejected earthly power and fame. He did not seek a throne, a following, or a movement based on personal glorification. He emptied himself, taking the form of a servant. He chose humility over recognition, sacrifice over success, and service over status.

In *The Gospel According to Donald Trump,* all of that is erased. Instead of a Messiah who lays down his life for others, we are left with a figure who demands loyalty, consolidates power, and pursues self-promotion at all costs.

A gospel centered on power and fame is no gospel at all.

Jesus Rejected Earthly Power—Trump Worships It

Jesus consistently distanced himself from political authority. He had every opportunity to seize power, yet he refused, saying "My kingdom is not of this world." (John 18:36)

After feeding the five thousand, the crowd tried to make him king by force. He fled. (John 6:15) When Satan tempted him in the wilderness, offering "all the kingdoms of the world and their splendor," Jesus rejected it outright. (Matthew 4:8-10)

When his disciples argued over who would be the greatest, Jesus didn't promise them thrones. He told them, "Whoever wants to be first must be last of all and servant of all." (Mark 9:35)

Trump operates by an entirely different philosophy:

"When somebody challenges you, fight back. Be brutal, be tough."

"I'm the most successful person ever to run for the presidency, by far."

"I alone can fix it."

Jesus' gospel is about self-denial. Trump's gospel is about self-glorification. In *The Gospel According to Donald Trump*, there is no retreat to the wilderness. There is no rejection of worldly power. There is no Kingdom of God that stands apart from the kingdoms of men. Instead, political dominance is the ultimate goal.

Jesus Shunned Fame—Trump Craves It

Jesus never sought personal fame. When he performed miracles, he often told people to stay silent about it. "Jesus warned them sternly, 'See that no one knows about this.'" (Matthew 9:30)

When crowds followed him for the spectacle, he rebuked them, "You are looking for me... because you ate the loaves and had your fill." (John 6:26)

Trump's entire identity, however, is built on fame as proof of success. He has attached his name to everything—skyscrapers, steaks, universities, casinos, even a Bible. He measures his worth in rally sizes, TV ratings, and applause.

Where Jesus withdrew from the crowds, Trump demands loyalty from them. Where Jesus warned against seeking the approval of men, Trump obsesses over adoration.

A gospel built on fame is a gospel devoid of substance. It is a brand, not a faith.

The Threat to the Gospel of Jesus Christ

The Gospel According to Donald Trump doesn't just compete with the gospel of Jesus—it undermines it. It replaces humility with self-glorification, sacrifice with self-interest, truth with power, love with loyalty tests, and servanthood with domination.

This distortion threatens the very core of Christianity. It leads to a faith where winning is more important than righteousness, where power is the goal and morality is the casualty, where the loudest, most aggressive, most ruthless leader is the one to be followed.

Jesus said, "You cannot serve both God and money." (Matthew 6:24) and "The greatest among you will be your servant." (Matthew 23:11)

But *The Gospel According to Donald Trump* preaches something else entirely. The greatest among you will be the most powerful. Blessed are the winners, for they shall own the losers. Loyalty matters more than truth."

A gospel that values fame over humility, power over sacrifice, and winning over righteousness is not the gospel of Jesus.

A False Gospel Cannot Save

By replacing humility with arrogance, servanthood with dominance, and love with self-glorification, *The Gospel According to Donald Trump* does not just distort Jesus' message—it reverses it.

A faith built on power and fame is not faith at all—it is idolatry.

And that is no gospel at all.

THE GOSPEL ACCORDING TO
DONALD TRUMP

www.ingramcontent.com/pod-product-compliance
Lightning Source LLC
Chambersburg PA
CBHW051339120626
46547CB00016B/2614